Mometrix TEST PREPARATION

Secrets of the

ACSM®

Certified Personal Trainer Exam Study Guide

I0880287

Dear Future Exam Success Story

First of all, **THANK YOU** for purchasing Mometrix study materials!

Second, congratulations! You are one of the few determined test-takers who are committed to doing whatever it takes to excel on your exam. **You have come to the right place.** We developed these study materials with one goal in mind: to deliver you the information you need in a format that's concise and easy to use.

In addition to optimizing your guide for the content of the test, we've outlined our recommended steps for breaking down the preparation process into small, attainable goals so you can make sure you stay on track.

We've also analyzed the entire test-taking process, identifying the most common pitfalls and showing how you can overcome them and be ready for any curveball the test throws you.

Standardized testing is one of the biggest obstacles on your road to success, which only increases the importance of doing well in the high-pressure, high-stakes environment of test day. Your results on this test could have a significant impact on your future, and this guide provides the information and practical advice to help you achieve your full potential on test day.

Your success is our success

We would love to hear from you! If you would like to share the story of your exam success or if you have any questions or comments in regard to our products, please contact us at **800-673-8175** or **support@mometrix.com**.

Thanks again for your business and we wish you continued success!

Sincerely,
The Mometrix Test Preparation Team

Need more help? Check out our flashcards at:
http://MometrixFlashcards.com/ACSM

Written and edited by the Mometrix Exam Secrets Test Prep Team
Printed in the United States of America

TABLE OF CONTENTS

Introduction

Thank you for purchasing this resource! You have made the choice to prepare yourself for a test that could have a huge impact on your future, and this guide is designed to help you be fully ready for test day. Obviously, it's important to have a solid understanding of the test material, but you also need to be prepared for the unique environment and stressors of the test, so that you can perform to the best of your abilities.

For this purpose, the first section that appears in this guide is the **Secret Keys**. We've devoted countless hours to meticulously researching what works and what doesn't, and we've boiled down our findings to the five most impactful steps you can take to improve your performance on the test. We start at the beginning with study planning and move through the preparation process, all the way to the testing strategies that will help you get the most out of what you know when you're finally sitting in front of the test.

We recommend that you start preparing for your test as far in advance as possible. However, if you've bought this guide as a last-minute study resource and only have a few days before your test, we recommend that you skip over the first two Secret Keys since they address a long-term study plan.

If you struggle with **test anxiety**, we strongly encourage you to check out our recommendations for how you can overcome it. Test anxiety is a formidable foe, but it can be beaten, and we want to make sure you have the tools you need to defeat it.

Secret Key #1 – Plan Big, Study Small

There's a lot riding on your performance. If you want to ace this test, you're going to need to keep your skills sharp and the material fresh in your mind. You need a plan that lets you review everything you need to know while still fitting in your schedule. We'll break this strategy down into three categories.

Information Organization

Start with the information you already have: the official test outline. From this, you can make a complete list of all the concepts you need to cover before the test. Organize these concepts into groups that can be studied together, and create a list of any related vocabulary you need to learn so you can brush up on any difficult terms. You'll want to keep this vocabulary list handy once you actually start studying since you may need to add to it along the way.

Time Management

Once you have your set of study concepts, decide how to spread them out over the time you have left before the test. Break your study plan into small, clear goals so you have a manageable task for each day and know exactly what you're doing. Then just focus on one small step at a time. When you manage your time this way, you don't need to spend hours at a time studying. Studying a small block of content for a short period each day helps you retain information better and avoid stressing over how much you have left to do. You can relax knowing that you have a plan to cover everything in time. In order for this strategy to be effective though, you have to start studying early and stick to your schedule. Avoid the exhaustion and futility that comes from last-minute cramming!

Study Environment

The environment you study in has a big impact on your learning. Studying in a coffee shop, while probably more enjoyable, is not likely to be as fruitful as studying in a quiet room. It's important to keep distractions to a minimum. You're only planning to study for a short block of time, so make the most of it. Don't pause to check your phone or get up to find a snack. It's also important to **avoid multitasking**. Research has consistently shown that multitasking will make your studying dramatically less effective. Your study area should also be comfortable and well-lit so you don't have the distraction of straining your eyes or sitting on an uncomfortable chair.

The time of day you study is also important. You want to be rested and alert. Don't wait until just before bedtime. Study when you'll be most likely to comprehend and remember. Even better, if you know what time of day your test will be, set that time aside for study. That way your brain will be used to working on that subject at that specific time and you'll have a better chance of recalling information.

Finally, it can be helpful to team up with others who are studying for the same test. Your actual studying should be done in as isolated an environment as possible, but the work of organizing the information and setting up the study plan can be divided up. In between study sessions, you can discuss with your teammates the concepts that you're all studying and quiz each other on the details. Just be sure that your teammates are as serious about the test as you are. If you find that your study time is being replaced with social time, you might need to find a new team.

Secret Key #2 – Make Your Studying Count

You're devoting a lot of time and effort to preparing for this test, so you want to be absolutely certain it will pay off. This means doing more than just reading the content and hoping you can remember it on test day. It's important to make every minute of study count. There are two main areas you can focus on to make your studying count.

Retention

It doesn't matter how much time you study if you can't remember the material. You need to make sure you are retaining the concepts. To check your retention of the information you're learning, try recalling it at later times with minimal prompting. Try carrying around flashcards and glance at one or two from time to time or ask a friend who's also studying for the test to quiz you.

To enhance your retention, look for ways to put the information into practice so that you can apply it rather than simply recalling it. If you're using the information in practical ways, it will be much easier to remember. Similarly, it helps to solidify a concept in your mind if you're not only reading it to yourself but also explaining it to someone else. Ask a friend to let you teach them about a concept you're a little shaky on (or speak aloud to an imaginary audience if necessary). As you try to summarize, define, give examples, and answer your friend's questions, you'll understand the concepts better and they will stay with you longer. Finally, step back for a big picture view and ask yourself how each piece of information fits with the whole subject. When you link the different concepts together and see them working together as a whole, it's easier to remember the individual components.

Finally, practice showing your work on any multi-step problems, even if you're just studying. Writing out each step you take to solve a problem will help solidify the process in your mind, and you'll be more likely to remember it during the test.

Modality

Modality simply refers to the means or method by which you study. Choosing a study modality that fits your own individual learning style is crucial. No two people learn best in exactly the same way, so it's important to know your strengths and use them to your advantage.

For example, if you learn best by visualization, focus on visualizing a concept in your mind and draw an image or a diagram. Try color-coding your notes, illustrating them, or creating symbols that will trigger your mind to recall a learned concept. If you learn best by hearing or discussing information, find a study partner who learns the same way or read aloud to yourself. Think about how to put the information in your own words. Imagine that you are giving a lecture on the topic and record yourself so you can listen to it later.

For any learning style, flashcards can be helpful. Organize the information so you can take advantage of spare moments to review. Underline key words or phrases. Use different colors for different categories. Mnemonic devices (such as creating a short list in which every item starts with the same letter) can also help with retention. Find what works best for you and use it to store the information in your mind most effectively and easily.

Secret Key #3 – Practice the Right Way

Your success on test day depends not only on how many hours you put into preparing, but also on whether you prepared the right way. It's good to check along the way to see if your studying is paying off. One of the most effective ways to do this is by taking practice tests to evaluate your progress. Practice tests are useful because they show exactly where you need to improve. Every time you take a practice test, pay special attention to these three groups of questions:

- The questions you got wrong
- The questions you had to guess on, even if you guessed right
- The questions you found difficult or slow to work through

This will show you exactly what your weak areas are, and where you need to devote more study time. Ask yourself why each of these questions gave you trouble. Was it because you didn't understand the material? Was it because you didn't remember the vocabulary? Do you need more repetitions on this type of question to build speed and confidence? Dig into those questions and figure out how you can strengthen your weak areas as you go back to review the material.

Additionally, many practice tests have a section explaining the answer choices. It can be tempting to read the explanation and think that you now have a good understanding of the concept. However, an explanation likely only covers part of the question's broader context. Even if the explanation makes perfect sense, **go back and investigate** every concept related to the question until you're positive you have a thorough understanding.

As you go along, keep in mind that the practice test is just that: practice. Memorizing these questions and answers will not be very helpful on the actual test because it is unlikely to have any of the same exact questions. If you only know the right answers to the sample questions, you won't be prepared for the real thing. **Study the concepts** until you understand them fully, and then you'll be able to answer any question that shows up on the test.

It's important to wait on the practice tests until you're ready. If you take a test on your first day of study, you may be overwhelmed by the amount of material covered and how much you need to learn. Work up to it gradually.

On test day, you'll need to be prepared for answering questions, managing your time, and using the test-taking strategies you've learned. It's a lot to balance, like a mental marathon that will have a big impact on your future. Like training for a marathon, you'll need to start slowly and work your way up. When test day arrives, you'll be ready.

Start with the strategies you've read in the first two Secret Keys—plan your course and study in the way that works best for you. If you have time, consider using multiple study resources to get different approaches to the same concepts. It can be helpful to see difficult concepts from more than one angle. Then find a good source for practice tests. Many times, the test website will suggest potential study resources or provide sample tests.

Practice Test Strategy

If you're able to find at least three practice tests, we recommend this strategy:

UNTIMED AND OPEN-BOOK PRACTICE

Take the first test with no time constraints and with your notes and study guide handy. Take your time and focus on applying the strategies you've learned.

TIMED AND OPEN-BOOK PRACTICE

Take the second practice test open-book as well, but set a timer and practice pacing yourself to finish in time.

TIMED AND CLOSED-BOOK PRACTICE

Take any other practice tests as if it were test day. Set a timer and put away your study materials. Sit at a table or desk in a quiet room, imagine yourself at the testing center, and answer questions as quickly and accurately as possible.

Keep repeating timed and closed-book tests on a regular basis until you run out of practice tests or it's time for the actual test. Your mind will be ready for the schedule and stress of test day, and you'll be able to focus on recalling the material you've learned.

Secret Key #4 – Pace Yourself

Once you're fully prepared for the material on the test, your biggest challenge on test day will be managing your time. Just knowing that the clock is ticking can make you panic even if you have plenty of time left. Work on pacing yourself so you can build confidence against the time constraints of the exam. Pacing is a difficult skill to master, especially in a high-pressure environment, so **practice is vital**.

Set time expectations for your pace based on how much time is available. For example, if a section has 60 questions and the time limit is 30 minutes, you know you have to average 30 seconds or less per question in order to answer them all. Although 30 seconds is the hard limit, set 25 seconds per question as your goal, so you reserve extra time to spend on harder questions. When you budget extra time for the harder questions, you no longer have any reason to stress when those questions take longer to answer.

Don't let this time expectation distract you from working through the test at a calm, steady pace, but keep it in mind so you don't spend too much time on any one question. Recognize that taking extra time on one question you don't understand may keep you from answering two that you do understand later in the test. If your time limit for a question is up and you're still not sure of the answer, mark it and move on, and come back to it later if the time and the test format allow. If the testing format doesn't allow you to return to earlier questions, just make an educated guess; then put it out of your mind and move on.

On the easier questions, be careful not to rush. It may seem wise to hurry through them so you have more time for the challenging ones, but it's not worth missing one if you know the concept and just didn't take the time to read the question fully. Work efficiently but make sure you understand the question and have looked at all of the answer choices, since more than one may seem right at first.

Even if you're paying attention to the time, you may find yourself a little behind at some point. You should speed up to get back on track, but do so wisely. Don't panic; just take a few seconds less on each question until you're caught up. Don't guess without thinking, but do look through the answer choices and eliminate any you know are wrong. If you can get down to two choices, it is often worthwhile to guess from those. Once you've chosen an answer, move on and don't dwell on any that you skipped or had to hurry through. If a question was taking too long, chances are it was one of the harder ones, so you weren't as likely to get it right anyway.

On the other hand, if you find yourself getting ahead of schedule, it may be beneficial to slow down a little. The more quickly you work, the more likely you are to make a careless mistake that will affect your score. You've budgeted time for each question, so don't be afraid to spend that time. Practice an efficient but careful pace to get the most out of the time you have.

Secret Key #5 – Have a Plan for Guessing

When you're taking the test, you may find yourself stuck on a question. Some of the answer choices seem better than others, but you don't see the one answer choice that is obviously correct. What do you do?

The scenario described above is very common, yet most test takers have not effectively prepared for it. Developing and practicing a plan for guessing may be one of the single most effective uses of your time as you get ready for the exam.

In developing your plan for guessing, there are three questions to address:

- When should you start the guessing process?
- How should you narrow down the choices?
- Which answer should you choose?

When to Start the Guessing Process

Unless your plan for guessing is to select C every time (which, despite its merits, is not what we recommend), you need to leave yourself enough time to apply your answer elimination strategies. Since you have a limited amount of time for each question, that means that if you're going to give yourself the best shot at guessing correctly, you have to decide quickly whether or not you will guess.

Of course, the best-case scenario is that you don't have to guess at all, so first, see if you can answer the question based on your knowledge of the subject and basic reasoning skills. Focus on the key words in the question and try to jog your memory of related topics. Give yourself a chance to bring the knowledge to mind, but once you realize that you don't have (or you can't access) the knowledge you need to answer the question, it's time to start the guessing process.

It's almost always better to start the guessing process too early than too late. It only takes a few seconds to remember something and answer the question from knowledge. Carefully eliminating wrong answer choices takes longer. Plus, going through the process of eliminating answer choices can actually help jog your memory.

Summary: Start the guessing process as soon as you decide that you can't answer the question based on your knowledge.

How to Narrow Down the Choices

The next chapter in this book (**Test-Taking Strategies**) includes a wide range of strategies for how to approach questions and how to look for answer choices to eliminate. You will definitely want to read those carefully, practice them, and figure out which ones work best for you. Here though, we're going to address a mindset rather than a particular strategy.

Your odds of guessing an answer correctly depend on how many options you are choosing from.

Number of options left	5	4	3	2	1
Odds of guessing correctly	20%	25%	33%	50%	100%

You can see from this chart just how valuable it is to be able to eliminate incorrect answers and make an educated guess, but there are two things that many test takers do that cause them to miss out on the benefits of guessing:

- Accidentally eliminating the correct answer
- Selecting an answer based on an impression

We'll look at the first one here, and the second one in the next section.

To avoid accidentally eliminating the correct answer, we recommend a thought exercise called **the $5 challenge**. In this challenge, you only eliminate an answer choice from contention if you are willing to bet $5 on it being wrong. Why $5? Five dollars is a small but not insignificant amount of money. It's an amount you could afford to lose but wouldn't want to throw away. And while losing $5 once might not hurt too much, doing it twenty times will set you back $100. In the same way, each small decision you make—eliminating a choice here, guessing on a question there—won't by itself impact your score very much, but when you put them all together, they can make a big difference. By holding each answer choice elimination decision to a higher standard, you can reduce the risk of accidentally eliminating the correct answer.

The $5 challenge can also be applied in a positive sense: If you are willing to bet $5 that an answer choice *is* correct, go ahead and mark it as correct.

Summary: Only eliminate an answer choice if you are willing to bet $5 that it is wrong.

Which Answer to Choose

You're taking the test. You've run into a hard question and decided you'll have to guess. You've eliminated all the answer choices you're willing to bet $5 on. Now you have to pick an answer. Why do we even need to talk about this? Why can't you just pick whichever one you feel like when the time comes?

The answer to these questions is that if you don't come into the test with a plan, you'll rely on your impression to select an answer choice, and if you do that, you risk falling into a trap. The test writers know that everyone who takes their test will be guessing on some of the questions, so they intentionally write wrong answer choices to seem plausible. You still have to pick an answer though, and if the wrong answer choices are designed to look right, how can you ever be sure that you're not falling for their trap? The best solution we've found to this dilemma is to take the decision out of your hands entirely. Here is the process we recommend:

Once you've eliminated any choices that you are confident (willing to bet $5) are wrong, select the first remaining choice as your answer.

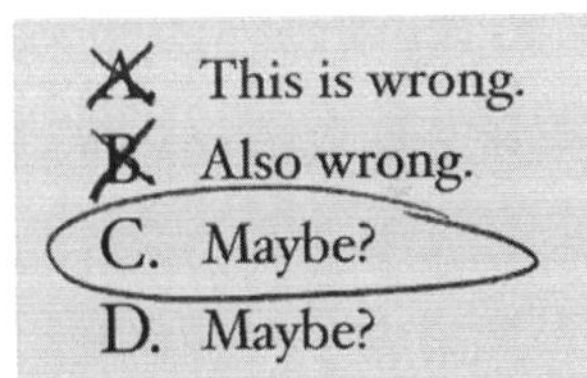

Whether you choose to select the first remaining choice, the second, or the last, the important thing is that you use some preselected standard. Using this approach guarantees that you will not be enticed into selecting an answer choice that looks right, because you are not basing your decision on how the answer choices look.

This is not meant to make you question your knowledge. Instead, it is to help you recognize the difference between your knowledge and your impressions. There's a huge difference between thinking an answer is right because of what you know, and thinking an answer is right because it looks or sounds like it should be right.

Summary: To ensure that your selection is appropriately random, make a predetermined selection from among all answer choices you have not eliminated.

Test-Taking Strategies

This section contains a list of test-taking strategies that you may find helpful as you work through the test. By taking what you know and applying logical thought, you can maximize your chances of answering any question correctly!

It is very important to realize that every question is different and every person is different: no single strategy will work on every question, and no single strategy will work for every person. That's why we've included all of them here, so you can try them out and determine which ones work best for different types of questions and which ones work best for you.

Question Strategies

☑ Read Carefully

Read the question and the answer choices carefully. Don't miss the question because you misread the terms. You have plenty of time to read each question thoroughly and make sure you understand what is being asked. Yet a happy medium must be attained, so don't waste too much time. You must read carefully and efficiently.

☑ Contextual Clues

Look for contextual clues. If the question includes a word you are not familiar with, look at the immediate context for some indication of what the word might mean. Contextual clues can often give you all the information you need to decipher the meaning of an unfamiliar word. Even if you can't determine the meaning, you may be able to narrow down the possibilities enough to make a solid guess at the answer to the question.

☑ Prefixes

If you're having trouble with a word in the question or answer choices, try dissecting it. Take advantage of every clue that the word might include. Prefixes can be a huge help. Usually, they allow you to determine a basic meaning. *Pre-* means before, *post-* means after, *pro-* is positive, *de-* is negative. From prefixes, you can get an idea of the general meaning of the word and try to put it into context.

☑ Hedge Words

Watch out for critical hedge words, such as *likely, may, can, often, almost, mostly, usually, generally, rarely,* and *sometimes.* Question writers insert these hedge phrases to cover every possibility. Often an answer choice will be wrong simply because it leaves no room for exception. Be on guard for answer choices that have definitive words such as *exactly* and *always.*

☑ Switchback Words

Stay alert for *switchbacks.* These are the words and phrases frequently used to alert you to shifts in thought. The most common switchback words are *but, although,* and *however.* Others include *nevertheless, on the other hand, even though, while, in spite of, despite,* and *regardless of.* Switchback words are important to catch because they can change the direction of the question or an answer choice.

✓ FACE VALUE

When in doubt, use common sense. Accept the situation in the problem at face value. Don't read too much into it. These problems will not require you to make wild assumptions. If you have to go beyond creativity and warp time or space in order to have an answer choice fit the question, then you should move on and consider the other answer choices. These are normal problems rooted in reality. The applicable relationship or explanation may not be readily apparent, but it is there for you to figure out. Use your common sense to interpret anything that isn't clear.

Answer Choice Strategies

✓ ANSWER SELECTION

The most thorough way to pick an answer choice is to identify and eliminate wrong answers until only one is left, then confirm it is the correct answer. Sometimes an answer choice may immediately seem right, but be careful. The test writers will usually put more than one reasonable answer choice on each question, so take a second to read all of them and make sure that the other choices are not equally obvious. As long as you have time left, it is better to read every answer choice than to pick the first one that looks right without checking the others.

✓ ANSWER CHOICE FAMILIES

An answer choice family consists of two (in rare cases, three) answer choices that are very similar in construction and cannot all be true at the same time. If you see two answer choices that are direct opposites or parallels, one of them is usually the correct answer. For instance, if one answer choice says that quantity *x* increases and another either says that quantity *x* decreases (opposite) or says that quantity *y* increases (parallel), then those answer choices would fall into the same family. An answer choice that doesn't match the construction of the answer choice family is more likely to be incorrect. Most questions will not have answer choice families, but when they do appear, you should be prepared to recognize them.

✓ ELIMINATE ANSWERS

Eliminate answer choices as soon as you realize they are wrong, but make sure you consider all possibilities. If you are eliminating answer choices and realize that the last one you are left with is also wrong, don't panic. Start over and consider each choice again. There may be something you missed the first time that you will realize on the second pass.

✓ AVOID FACT TRAPS

Don't be distracted by an answer choice that is factually true but doesn't answer the question. You are looking for the choice that answers the question. Stay focused on what the question is asking for so you don't accidentally pick an answer that is true but incorrect. Always go back to the question and make sure the answer choice you've selected actually answers the question and is not merely a true statement.

✓ EXTREME STATEMENTS

In general, you should avoid answers that put forth extreme actions as standard practice or proclaim controversial ideas as established fact. An answer choice that states the "process should be used in certain situations, if..." is much more likely to be correct than one that states the "process should be discontinued completely." The first is a calm rational statement and doesn't even make a definitive, uncompromising stance, using a hedge word *if* to provide wiggle room, whereas the second choice is far more extreme.

☑ BENCHMARK

As you read through the answer choices and you come across one that seems to answer the question well, mentally select that answer choice. This is not your final answer, but it's the one that will help you evaluate the other answer choices. The one that you selected is your benchmark or standard for judging each of the other answer choices. Every other answer choice must be compared to your benchmark. That choice is correct until proven otherwise by another answer choice beating it. If you find a better answer, then that one becomes your new benchmark. Once you've decided that no other choice answers the question as well as your benchmark, you have your final answer.

☑ PREDICT THE ANSWER

Before you even start looking at the answer choices, it is often best to try to predict the answer. When you come up with the answer on your own, it is easier to avoid distractions and traps because you will know exactly what to look for. The right answer choice is unlikely to be word-for-word what you came up with, but it should be a close match. Even if you are confident that you have the right answer, you should still take the time to read each option before moving on.

General Strategies

☑ TOUGH QUESTIONS

If you are stumped on a problem or it appears too hard or too difficult, don't waste time. Move on! Remember though, if you can quickly check for obviously incorrect answer choices, your chances of guessing correctly are greatly improved. Before you completely give up, at least try to knock out a couple of possible answers. Eliminate what you can and then guess at the remaining answer choices before moving on.

☑ CHECK YOUR WORK

Since you will probably not know every term listed and the answer to every question, it is important that you get credit for the ones that you do know. Don't miss any questions through careless mistakes. If at all possible, try to take a second to look back over your answer selection and make sure you've selected the correct answer choice and haven't made a costly careless mistake (such as marking an answer choice that you didn't mean to mark). This quick double check should more than pay for itself in caught mistakes for the time it costs.

☑ PACE YOURSELF

It's easy to be overwhelmed when you're looking at a page full of questions; your mind is confused and full of random thoughts, and the clock is ticking down faster than you would like. Calm down and maintain the pace that you have set for yourself. Especially as you get down to the last few minutes of the test, don't let the small numbers on the clock make you panic. As long as you are on track by monitoring your pace, you are guaranteed to have time for each question.

☑ DON'T RUSH

It is very easy to make errors when you are in a hurry. Maintaining a fast pace in answering questions is pointless if it makes you miss questions that you would have gotten right otherwise. Test writers like to include distracting information and wrong answers that seem right. Taking a little extra time to avoid careless mistakes can make all the difference in your test score. Find a pace that allows you to be confident in the answers that you select.

⊘ Keep Moving

Panicking will not help you pass the test, so do your best to stay calm and keep moving. Taking deep breaths and going through the answer elimination steps you practiced can help to break through a stress barrier and keep your pace.

Final Notes

The combination of a solid foundation of content knowledge and the confidence that comes from practicing your plan for applying that knowledge is the key to maximizing your performance on test day. As your foundation of content knowledge is built up and strengthened, you'll find that the strategies included in this chapter become more and more effective in helping you quickly sift through the distractions and traps of the test to isolate the correct answer.

Now that you're preparing to move forward into the test content chapters of this book, be sure to keep your goal in mind. As you read, think about how you will be able to apply this information on the test. If you've already seen sample questions for the test and you have an idea of the question format and style, try to come up with questions of your own that you can answer based on what you're reading. This will give you valuable practice applying your knowledge in the same ways you can expect to on test day.

Good luck and good studying!

Initial Client Consultation and Assessment

Preparing for Initial Potential Client Visit

The goal of the first session should be to make a positive first impression, establish expectations, and create a blueprint for success. The first session with a client lays the foundation for a successful relationship, and adequate preparation ensures a successful initial meeting. When preparing for an initial client consultation, the personal trainer should gather the necessary items in advance to facilitate a productive session. Relevant materials include:

- client documents
- client and trainer expectations
- pricing information
- payment expectations (i.e., when payment is due, and what forms of payment are accepted)
- cancellation policy (the personal trainer should clearly identify the cutoff point for canceling a session without incurring a fee)

The initial consultation should include a tour of the fitness facilities. The trainer should advise the client of equipment that the client needs to purchase before the first training session (i.e., proper exercise clothing and footwear). The client should clearly understand what will happen at the first session and when the paperwork is due, especially if medical clearance is required.

Paperwork

The personal trainer must have the client fill out the following paperwork:

- Health History Questionnaire
- Par-Q & You
- Client Participation Contract

The client should complete required paperwork before exercise testing. The Health History Questionnaire should inquire about a client's medical history, current health status, and family medical history. If a response indicates a potential medical condition, the client should be referred to a physician. The Par-Q and You is a health screening tool that determines a client's readiness to begin an exercise program. It consists of 7 yes or no questions. If the client answers yes to any of the questions, they should consult a physician before they begin an exercise program. It is imperative for the trainer to instruct the client to obtain clearance from a physician before undertaking an exercise routine if the Par-Q & You and the Health History Questionnaire raise any red flags. It is a professional obligation to inform medical staff intimately involved with a client's ongoing care of potential exercise plans.

The Client Participation Contract is designed to inform the client of any potential risks associated with exercising and serves as an agreement that the client is willingly participating in the program. The personal trainer must decide if any other contracts or agreements require a signature (e.g., a payment agreement form, medical clearance form).

Performing a Client Interview

Effectively Communicating Expectations

At the initial client session, the personal trainer must clearly communicate expectations for the client. Expectations to discuss include timeliness, dress, and expected level of exertion/discomfort. The trainer should share expectations in an encouraging way and use positive nonverbal communication (e.g. eye contact, smiling, a tone of voice that is kind, but firm). Communicate that continuously establishing goals and assessing progress are crucial components of a training program. Give the client time to ask questions. Establish that the client should feel free to ask questions at any time and participate in future goal setting.

Proper Communication

The trainer can communicate verbally or nonverbally using a variety of mediums. Verbal communication is the primary method of interacting in the club. It is important to consider eye contact, tone of voice, and gestures when communicating with a client verbally. The telephone is a way to communicate verbally when the client is outside of the club. Written communication in the form of email or text is an excellent way to convey information to the client if the message is not time sensitive. Newsletters, handouts, articles, and brochures spread general information to a broad audience. The personal trainer needs to consider principles of confidentiality and should only share client information with third parties if the client has given written consent. Only place calls and send texts from a personal phone as a last resort to ensure a professional working relationship with clients.

Prescreening Clients Before Exercise Instruction

It is important to prescreen clients to assess their medical risk. Setting appropriate goals and designing training sessions requires an assessment of medical risk. Understanding the client's medical risk factors helps the personal trainer determine if medical consent is required before the client starts a training program. The most common forms used by personal trainers include the following: health/medical history questionnaire, informed consent, trainer-client contract, and policies/procedures.

- The Par-Q & You (or a general health questionnaire) is a health/medical history questionnaire that assesses common risk factors related to exercise and indicates whether a client requires medical clearance.
- Informed consent ensures the client understands the relative risks and discomforts associated with exercise sessions.
- The trainer-client contract outlines the number of sessions and covers pricing considerations. The trainer and the client sin this document.
- Policies and procedures are the guiding principles that result in a positive experience for the client. Policies are statements of intent outlining the company's conduct. Procedures are the action plan used to implement the policies. Policies and procedures can include guidelines for missed sessions, cancellation policy, and appropriate dress.

Medical Clearance

If the client is over 40 and has been inactive for a substantial time period, or answers yes to any questions on the Par-Q & You form, medical clearance is necessary before the client participates in an exercise program. If the client has an untreated medical condition, make a note of the condition, and inform the client's physician of the issue. Depending on the conditions present in the client, written permission from the physician may be sufficient; however, certain cardiovascular issues may require a physician administered stress test. The client must obtain medical clearance before the initial exercise testing for any known issues (or issues covered by Par-Q & You form). A medical issue may arise during the initial exercise testing or in subsequent sessions. If this is the case, refer the client to a physician and request medical clearance before resuming the program.

Use of Screening Information to Develop Overall Goals

Initial screening information includes information gathered from both the paperwork and fitness testing of the client. The personal trainer ascertains the client's personal goals, motivation level, and health challenges from the paperwork. The personal trainer evaluates physiological deficiencies in the client's training with fitness testing. Develop client goals according to identified deficiencies. The program addresses the greatest deficiencies first; lesser deficiencies are tackled after progress has been made on the most pressing issues. Connect specific goals for each area of weakness and explain how the goal improves the deficiency. Create a goal that is measurable and attainable. Creating a measurable and attainable goal requires the development of a rubric to assess client progress at regular intervals.

Overview of Fitness Facility and Equipment

It is up to the personal trainer to ensure that the client understands how to use equipment in the training facility properly. The client can demonstrate proper equipment use in various ways. The trainer must take the client on a tour of the fitness center so they can become oriented with the location of important amenities (i.e., locker rooms, bathrooms, equipment rooms, towels, etc.). The trainer must communicate expectations for each exercise session using verbal and nonverbal cues and by demonstrating the movement. Give the client time to ask questions about equipment usage. Ensuring the client knows how to use the equipment independently allows the client to work out at the fitness center without trainer supervision.

Dangers of Beginning a Training Regimen Without Proper Paperwork on File

It is never advisable to train a client before the paperwork is completed and signed. A completed health history form reduces the risk of complications arising during training sessions. Medical clearance and informed consent forms protect the trainer from liability issues. Without clearly outlined policies and procedures that establish session expectations, the trainer-client relationship can suffer. Finally, without paperwork, the trainer is unable to create and communicate effective goals for the client.

Reviewing and Analyzing Client Data

Familiarity with ACSM Risk Factors

Familiarity with the ACSM risk factors for cardiovascular, pulmonary, and metabolic diseases is crucial for the personal trainer. Knowledge of risk factors is necessary to analyze the paperwork completed by the client at the initial meeting. Risk factor awareness allows the trainer to stratify the client's risk, which is a crucial component of the goal-setting process. The trainer will be unable to determine if the client requires additional medical clearance to participate in an exercise program without an understanding of risk factors. Being well-versed in the various risk factors allows the trainer to identify potentially dangerous symptoms, evaluate the program, and make adjustments as needed to ensure client safety. The common risk factors recognized by the ACSM include:

- Family history
- Cigarette smoking
- Hypertension (high blood pressure)
- Hypercholesterolemia (high cholesterol)
- Impaired fasting glucose
- Obesity
- Sedentary lifestyle

A client who demonstrates one or more of the following risk factors may be at risk of cardiovascular, pulmonary, and metabolic diseases, and ACSM reccommends that these clients receive medical clearance prior to beginning an exercise regimen.

Possible Symptoms of Disease

Chronic Cardiovascular Disease

Clients should be observed for symptoms of coronary artery disease and cardiovascular disease, as both can be common. Symptoms include high blood pressure, high cholesterol, high blood sugar, a sedentary lifestyle, smoking (current or past history), and family history of heart attack or coronary revascularization or sudden death. Blood pressure is a measurement of the force exerted by the blood on the interior walls of the arteries. Blood pressure emanates from the heart, which pumps the blood throughout the body. A stethoscope (to listen to the pulse at the brachial artery) and a sphygmomanometer (cuffed around the arm, above the elbow) measure blood pressure). To take a blood pressure reading, rapidly inflate the cuff to 20–30 mm Hg above the point at which the pulse at the wrist is undetectable. Release the pressure at 2 mm Hg per second. The systolic reading is the top number of a blood pressure measurement. The systolic reading registers when the pressure releases and the sound of the pulse is audible. It reflects the maximum force produced by the cardiac cycle. The diastolic reading records when the sound of the pulse fades away. It appears on the bottom of the reading and reflects the lowest amount of pressure produced during the cardiac cycle. A normal reading for an adult is between 120 to 130 mm Hg for the systolic number and from 80 to 85 mm Hg for the diastolic number. High cholesterol is defined as having an HDL reading of <40 mg/dl and a LDL of >130 mg/dl with high triglyceride levels and requires a medical test to determine. High blood sugar is defined as a fasting blood glucose level of >60 mg/dl and requires a medical test to determine. Elevated blood sugar that is not controlled has myriad negative side effects on the body. Obesity is a clinical term defined as the class of people who have a body mass index (BMI) of 30 or greater. BMI is calculated by taking a person's metric weight (in kilograms) and dividing it by their metric height (in meters) squared. Morbid obesity is considered to be a BMI greater than 40. An individual with a BMI reading less than 18.5 is considered underweight. A BMI reading between 18.5 and 24.9 falls within the healthy range. Clients with BMI readings between 25 and 30 have an overweight designation. A person who rarely or never exercises is said to live a sedentary lifestyle which poses many health risks. Smoking poses many health risks, clients with a history of smoking may have health issues to address and current smokers should be encouraged to quit. It is important to consider a client's family history when evaluating a client. A family history of heart attack or coronary revascularization or sudden death (in a male age 55 or under who is a father or immediate relative, in a female age 65 or under who is a mother or immediate relative). The Health History Questionnaire clearly indicates the risk factors for the personal trainer to observe. The following symptoms can be observed in clients who may be at risk for cardiovascular disease:

- a lack of adequate circulation which can lead to pain or discomfort in the arms, chest, neck, or jaw
- experiencing shortness of breath even though not expending a high amount of energy or effort
- dizziness or fainting spells
- experiencing discomfort during breathing when lying down or at night
- swelling of the ankles
- heart palpitations (abnormal heart beat
- tachycardia (rapid heartbeat)
- cramping and sensations of weakness in the legs when walking
- heart murmur
- unusual levels of fatigue

Chronic Pulmonary Disease

The symptoms indicating pulmonary disease are similar to those indicating cardiovascular disease and are as follows:

- a lack of adequate circulation which can lead to pain or discomfort in the arms, chest, neck, or jaw
- experiencing shortness of breath even though not expending a high amount of energy or effort
- dizziness or fainting (syncope) spells
- experiencing discomfort during breathing when lying down (orthopnea) or at night (nocturnal dyspnea)
- swelling (edema) of the ankles
- heart palpitations (abnormal heartbeat)
- tachycardia (rapid heartbeat)
- cramping and sensations of weakness in the legs when walking
- heart murmur
- unusual levels of fatigue

Since indications are similar between the two conditions, it is of paramount importance to be in close contact with medical personnel to relay your observations.

Chronic Metabolic Disease

The following symptoms may indicate that a client has metabolic disease:

- excess abdominal fat (women: waist circumference > 88cm, men: waist circumference > 102cm)
- high triglyceride levels (> 150mg/dl), low HDL cholesterol (< 40mg/dl); (typically determined by a doctor)
- high fasting glucose levels (> 110mg/dl); (typically determined by a doctor)
- high blood pressure (> 130/85 mmHg). (typically determined by a doctor)

Types of metabolic disease have traditionally included Type 1 and 2 Diabetes, although any disease that interferes with the metabolic processing of nutrients that enter the body is considered metabolic disease. The list also includes diseases such as polycystic ovarian syndrome, dementia, cancer, and fatty liver (not due to excess alcohol consumption).

ACSM Model for Risk Stratification

The ACSM risk stratification model identifies several areas for the personal trainer to assess. The personal trainer makes a list of the positive and negative risk factors when assessing risk. Place the client in either a low-, moderate-, or high-risk stratum. To be considered in the low-risk stratum, the client must be younger, asymptomatic, or meet only one of the risk factors for cardiovascular or pulmonary disease. To be considered in the moderate-risk stratum, the client must be older (men aged >45, women aged >55) and meet the lower threshold of no more than two of the risk factors for cardiovascular or pulmonary disease. To be considered in the high-risk stratum, the client must have known disease (cardiovascular, pulmonary, or metabolic) or have one of the risk factors indicating cardiovascular or pulmonary disease. A physician should supervise moderate and high-risk clients before a trainer conducts maximal exercise testing. Clients at low and moderate risk may safely engage in submaximal exercise testing.

Risk Level	Applies to:	Criteria
Low risk	Asymptomatic men and women	Have ≤1 CVD risk factors
Moderate risk	Asymptomatic men and women	Have ≥2 CVD risk factors
High risk	Individuals with a known cardiovascular, pulmonary, or metabolic disease or that have any signs and symptoms those diseases.	

ACSM Risk Factor		Defining Criteria
Positive Risk Factors	Family history	Myocardial infarction, coronary revascularization, or sudden death before 55 yr. of age in father or other male first-degree relative, or before 65 yr. of age in mother or other female first-degree relative
	Cigarette smoking	Current cigarette smoker or those who quit within the previous 6 months or exposure to environmental tobacco smoke
	Sedentary lifestyle	Not participating in at least 30 min of moderate intensity physical activity on at least three days of the week for at least three months
	Obesity	Body mass index ≥30 kg·m2 or waist girth >102 cm (40 inches) for men and >88 cm (35 inches) for women
	Hypertension	Systolic blood pressure ≥140 mm Hg and/or diastolic ≥90 mm Hg, confirmed by measurements on at least two separate occasions, or on antihypertensive medication
	Dyslipidemia	Low-density lipoprotein (LDL-C) cholesterol ≥130 mg·dL-1 (3.37 mmol·L-1) or high-density lipoprotein (HDL-C) cholesterol <40 mg·dL-1 (1.04 mmol·L-1) or on lipid-lowering medication. If total serum cholesterol is all that is available, use ≥200 mg·dL-1 (5.18 mmol·L-1)
	Prediabetes	Impaired fasting glucose (IFG) = fasting plasma glucose ≥100 mg·dL-1 (5.50 mmol·L-1) but <126 mg·dL-1 (6.93 mmol·L-1) or impaired glucose tolerance (IGT) = 2-hour values in oral glucose tolerance test (OGTT) ≥140 mg·dL-1 (7.70 mmol· L-1) but <200 mg·dL-1 (11.00 mmol·L-1) confirmed by measurements on at least two separate occasions
Negative Risk Factor	High-serum HDL cholesterol	≥60 mg·dL-1 (1.55 mmol·L-1)

It is imperative for the personal trainer to know and utilize the ACSM guidelines for risk stratification. The personal trainer must understand that assessment is an ongoing process. The primary purpose of the ACSM guidelines is to promote safety. It is a preventative action designed to limit risk and reduce liability. It assists the trainer to design a program that allows the client to exercise safely while still enjoying results.

Plan of Action If Symptoms of Disease Are Observed

If the client shows symptoms of a chronic cardiovascular, pulmonary, or metabolic tendency after completing the initial paperwork, the personal trainer must communicate the findings to the client and explain the risks. The personal trainer must refer the client for medical attention and request that the client receives medical permission to exercise before resuming sessions. If the client is already under medical supervision, it is appropriate for the personal trainer to call the primary physician to discuss the client's fitness plans. It is best to receive medical permission to exercise from the doctor in writing so the trainer can limit personal liability.

Creating an Exercise Program

The personal trainer must take all initial paperwork and the initial exercise testing and observe the following: health risks; lifestyle behaviors; basic nutritional habits; positive behaviors; personal goals; baseline levels of muscular endurance, strength, and power; flexibility; and level of cardiovascular fitness. Next, the trainer should create a list of goals according to the greatest deficiencies in the client's lifestyle and fitness level. The trainer needs to include issues that the client wants to improve as well. Each session should aim to meet one or more of the goals. The amount of time allotted to each goal directly proportional to the greatest area of deficiency.

Communication with Medical Personnel

If the results of the health history questionnaire indicate that the client should seek medical care, or if the client is already under a physician's care, and still shows significant risk after the risk stratification process, it is up to the personal trainer to contact the physician. The trainer must be prepared to discuss exercise plans with the physician and schedule updates on client progress with the physician. The personal trainer must be prepared to provide detailed written, electronic, or verbal communication about the client's fitness progress depending on the physician's desired level of involvement.

Evaluating Behavioral Readiness

Health Behavior Change Models

The client can experience lasting change with the support of family and friends. The personal trainer must help the client understand how to troubleshoot and identify ways to prevent self-sabotaging the ability to change. It is important to teach methods that prevent self-sabotage to provide the client with the best chance of meeting goals. IKnowledge of health behavior change models allows the trainer to reinforce positive behaviors. Some examples of health behavior change models are as follows:

- The socio-ecologic model: This model helps the trainer understand the different variables affecting a client's motivation to move. Often the client has been motivated by national trends or news, or community/organizational/family relationships. These areas can positively or negatively affect the client's continuing change.
- Readiness to change model: The client has passed through one or more of the stages of change (i.e. pre-contemplation, contemplation, preparation, action, motivation). Identifying a client's position on the continuum helps the trainer apply the proper motivational techniques.
- Social cognitive theory: The theory asserts that learning occurs in a social context with observation being the primary means of learning.
- Theory of planned behavior: Three different types of beliefs—behavioral, normative, and control beliefs—motivate behavior.

Goal Setting

The purpose of setting goals is to identify what you want to accomplish. The benefits of goals are purpose, focus, accountability, and motivation. With such an important role to fill, ACSM recommends using the SMART method which serves as a guide for health and fitness professionals to use when creating a strategy for each client to achieve his or her fitness goals. The letters stand for the following:

- Specific—A specific goal clearly identifies what is to be achieved. Specific goals offer clear direction and level set expectations.
- Measurable—Measurable goals can be quantified and tracked. Without the ability to track goals, it is difficult to determine success or failure.
- Attainable—An attainable goal follows the Goldilocks principle (not too easy not too hard). It is challenging enough that the client must work hard to achieve it, but not so difficult that the client loses hope. Clients do not progress when goals are too easy and lose motivation when goals are not attainable.
- Realistic—A goal is realistic if a client is willing and able to achieve it.
- Timely— Time-bound goals have clearly defined time frames which provide structure and set priorities.

Each exercise session should clearly align with a goal. There should be one goal for each area of fitness (cardiovascular, muscular strength/power/endurance, and flexibility) to promote simplicity. The number of contracted sessions determines how many times the goals will be assessed. Goal assessment needs to occur at regular intervals, so the client sees progress clearly. Goals will set the tone and provide purpose for the workouts. Clearly communicate expectations to the client to demonstrate how each session is important to the overall picture of his health.

Realistic Goals to Reinforce Positive Behavior Change

When goals are realistic, the client achieves them promptly. When a client equates achieving goals with health gains, commitment to the program increases. Setting a realistic goal builds the client's confidence to make positive changes, which increases the motivation to tackle more challenging goals.

Social Support

Social support from organizations, family, and friends can help a client change negative behaviors into positive ones. For instance, a client's workplace or health insurance may offer incentives that reward becoming part of a fitness center, exercising regularly, or getting nutritional counseling. Family and friends can provide emotional support that motivates a client to move past the discomfort of fitness so they can achieve results. An unhealthy work environment or negative feedback from family and friends can discourage a client from maintaining new positive habits. In this case, the personal trainer needs to provide the motivation and encouragement that will not be found in other places.

Goals for Fitness Components

Cardiovascular endurance: ACSM defines cardiovascular endurance as the ability to perform prolonged aerobic exercise at moderate to high exercise intensities and states that cardiovascular endurance is highly related to the functioning of the lungs, heart, and circulatory system and the capacity of skeletal muscle to extract oxygen and thereby sustain performance. Cardiovascular endurance goals can be measured using distance, time, heart rate, or Vo2max. An example of a cardiovascular endurance goal is "the client will build the stamina to run 1 mile without stopping to walk within the next 3 weeks".

Muscular strength: Muscular strength is defined by ACSM as the maximal amount of force one can generate during a specific movement pattern at a specified velocity of contraction. Muscular strength is commonly measured by the one repetition maximum (1RM). An example of a muscular strength goal is "the client will develop the ability to hold the plank position for 1 full minute within the next 2 weeks".

Muscular endurance: ACSM defines muscular endurance as the ability to sustain performance and resist fatigue. Muscular endurance is typically measured in volume of work completed. Completing a greater volume of work, or reducing the amount of rest in between sets are measures of muscular endurance. An example of a muscular endurance goal is "the client will build the strength to perform 50 curl-ups in 1 minute within the next 3 weeks".

Muscular power: ACSM defines muscular power is the rate of performing work and states that because power is the product of force and velocity, there is a strength component to power development (strength at low-to-high velocities of contraction) Power is measured by rate of force production and can be expressed by velocity generated or in elapsed time. Increased velocity generated and completing the movement in a shorter period of time are evidence that power has increased. An example of muscular power is "The client will be able to complete 3 sets of jump squats, single leg hops, and hurdles in 20 minutes within the next month".

Flexibility: Flexibility is defined by ACSM as the ability of a joint to move freely through its range of motion. Joint flexibility is measured using a variety of tests that demonstrate range of motion. Improvement in the tests demonstrates improved flexibility. "The client will develop the flexibility to touch the floor in the double leg hamstring stretch within the next month" is an example of a flexibility goal.

Body fat assessment: According to ACSM body composition refers to the proportion of fat and fat-free mass throughout the body. Fat-free mass (or lean body mass) is that component consisting of bone,muscle, water, and other nonfat tissues. Bondy composition is commonly measured by BMI and body fat percentage. An example of a body composition goal is "the client will reduce total body fat by 2% within the next month".

Skill-Related Fitness Components

ACSM recognizes speed, agility, reaction time, and balance and coordination as fitness components that require skill. Speed is defied by ACSM as the capacity of an individual to perform a motor skill as rapidly as possible. ACSM defines agility as the ability of an individual to change direction rapidly without a significant loss of speed, balance, or bodily control. According to ACSM, reaction time is the ability to respond rapidly to a stimulus. Balance is the ability of an individual to maintain equilibrium as defined by ACSM. Coordination is defined by ACSM as the ability of an individual to perform a motor skill with good technique, rhythm, and accuracy. It is important for the trainer to design a component that aims to improve these fitness elements.

Assessing Physical Fitness

Structure of Bones, Skeletal Muscle, and Connective Tissue

Most of the bones of the appendicular skeleton have an epiphysis (head) and a diaphysis (shaft). There is also an outer layer of the bone (periosteum) and an inner layer of the bone (endosteum). Spongy bone can be found inside the epiphysis of the bone and contains blood vessels. Articular cartilage can be found outside the epiphysis at the connecting site of a joint. Skeletal muscle is striated with multiple nuclei. It most often has bony attachments and is voluntary. There are three types of connective tissue: loose (includes areolar, adipose, and reticular), dense (includes dense regular and dense irregular), and cartilage (hyaline, elastic, and fibrocartilage).

The skeleton provides a support system for the muscles and organs of the body and initiates movement. Additionally, the skeletal system protects major organs (heart, brain, etc.) and creates red blood cells (this takes place in the bone marrow). The skeletal system stores minerals (such as calcium and phosphorus) and releases them into the body, which regulates mineral balance and promotes proper body function.

The skeletal system contains two major sections: the axial skeletal system and the appendicular skeletal system. The axial skeletal system has nearly 80 bones and is composed of the head, spine, and rib cage. The appendicular system contains the appendages, the shoulders, and the hip complex. It has more than 120 bones.

SKELETAL SYSTEM

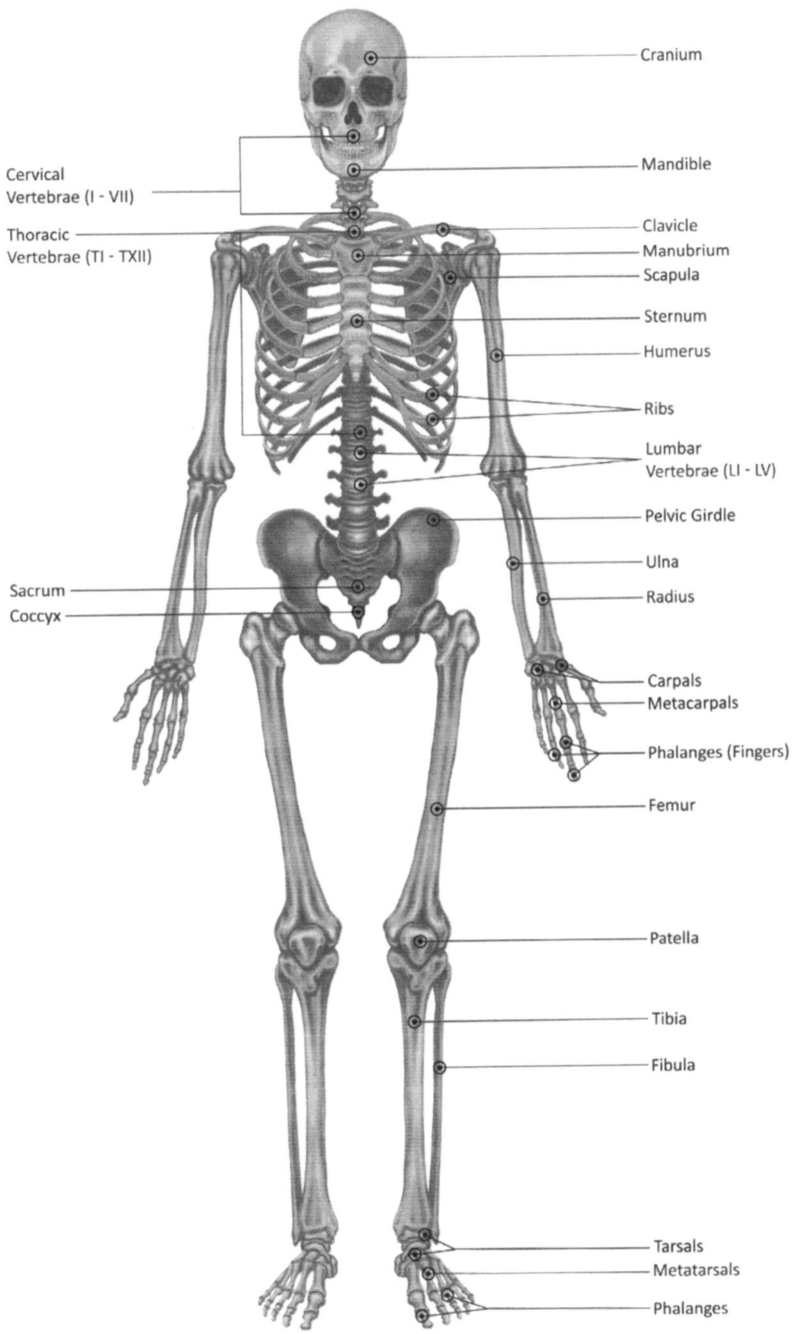

The two types of tissue that exist within human bones are compact bone and spongy bone. Compact bone resides on the outer layer of bones (the surface). Compact bone is very tough and serves a protective function by allowing the bone to bear the entire weight of the body. Spongy bone contains more spaces than compact bone and houses bone marrow.

The skeleton is composed of long bones, short bones, flat bones, irregular bones, and sesamoid (round) bones. Examples of long bones are the humerus and the femur. The shaft of a long bone, which is called the diaphysis, is made up of compact bone. The ends of a long bone are called the epiphyses, and these are made up of cancellous bone. The epiphyses are the sites of bone growth. Short bones are found in groups, and aid in movement. This type of bone is found in the wrist and ankle. Examples of flat bones are the ribs, scapula, sternum, and cranial bones. The vertebrae, facial bones, and skull bones are irregular bones. Sesamoid bones are located within a tendon. The patella, for example, is a sesamoid bone.

Review Video: Skeletal System
Visit mometrix.com/academy and enter code: 256447

Bone Markings

Every bone has markings on its exterior that serve various functions. One major function is to provide place for muscles or other connective tissue to attach. There are two major categories of bone markings: processes and depressions.

Processes are bulges that protrude from the bone. Some examples include the rounded ends of the femur or humerus. Listed here are examples of bone processes:

- Trochanters—the rounded end of the femur; the hip bone is known as the greater trochanter.
- Tubercles—the top of the humerus; there are tubercles in the shoulder complex also.
- Condyles—the bottom of the femur, where condyles help form the knee joint.
- Epicondyles—the bottom of the humerus, where epicondyles help form the elbow joint.

Depressions are parts of the bone that are smooth or flat. Common depressions are the fossa or sulcus. These are locations where muscle or body tissues can attach or pass between.

Skeletal Muscle

The three different types of muscle tissue are cardiac, smooth, and skeletal. The heart is composed of cardiac muscle. Organs (e.g., the liver or kidneys) contain smooth muscle. Skeletal muscle attaches to the skeletal system. Examples of skeletal muscle include the deltoid and trapezius muscles. The central nervous system (CNS) controls cardiac and smooth muscle with automatic processes. Skeletal muscle appears striated is voluntary control of the CNS.

Connective Tissue

Connective tissue connects muscles or bones together throughout the body. Tendons connect muscle to bone, and ligaments connect bone to bone. Both tendons and ligaments (dense regular connective tissue) serve a protective function by holding muscles and bones in their proper place and aiding in proper range of motion. When tendons and ligaments stretch beyond their capacity, an injury can occur. The personal trainer must understand that working muscles and their corresponding joints outside of their normal range of motion can cause excess stretching in the ligaments and possible damage. In addition, overuse injuries and excessive repetitive force can cause tendon damage. The trainer must be aware of preexisting weaknesses in connective tissue before proceeding to a training program with a client. Loose connective tissue can be found around the organs (areolar), under the skin (adipose), and in bone marrow (reticular). Cartilage can be found in the ribs/nose/trachea/larynx (hyaline), external ear (elastic), and in vertebral discs and knees (fibrocartilage).

Anatomy of Cardiovascular and Respiratory Systems

The basic anatomy of the cardiovascular system is as follows: heart (right and left atrium, right and left ventricle, bicuspid valve, tricuspid valve, pulmonary semilunar valve, aortic semilunar valve, aorta, superior and inferior vena cava) and blood vessels (arteries, arterioles, veins, venules, capillaries). The basic anatomy of the respiratory system is as follows: nose, sinuses, pharynx, larynx, trachea, bronchi, bronchioles, alveoli. Blood that is deoxygenated flows through the superior and inferior vena cava into the right atrium. The right atrium contracts, pushing blood through the tricuspid valve and into the right ventricle. The right ventricle then contracts, the tricuspid valve closes, and the blood is forced through the pulmonary semilunar valve. The pulmonary arteries carry the blood into the alveolar capillaries where oxygen is absorbed, and carbon dioxide is removed. The pulmonary veins carry blood back to the left atrium. The left atrium contracts and the blood moves into the left ventricle through the bicuspid valve. The left ventricle contracts and the bicuspid valve closes; blood then is forced into the aortic valve where it goes into coronary and systemic circulation.

Cardiovascular System

The elements in the body that create and circulate blood (e.g., the heart, the blood, the veins, and the capillaries) comprise the cardiovascular system.

The cardiovascular system has several functions. It removes metabolic waste from and delivers nutrients to the body. White blood cells provide protection from foreign microbes and viruses. Finally, the cardiovascular system helps keep our bodies in a state of homeostasis by controlling body temperature, pH balance, and cellular water retention.

Blood and Channels of Blood Distribution

Blood is the liquid that flows throughout the body, carrying out several functions. The average person has about 1.5 gallons of blood circulating at one time, and blood makes up a little less than 10 percent of a person's overall weight on average. Blood:

- carries oxygen and nutrients to the body systems
- acts as a conduit to rid the body of waste products
- regulates the body, helping keep body temperature constant and maintaining acid balance
- is a defensive mechanism, clotting when necessary to prevent bleeding and creating and circulating defensive cells to help fight infection

The cardiovascular system circulates five liters of blood through the body. It takes approximately one minute for a red blood cell to make its way through the entire human body.

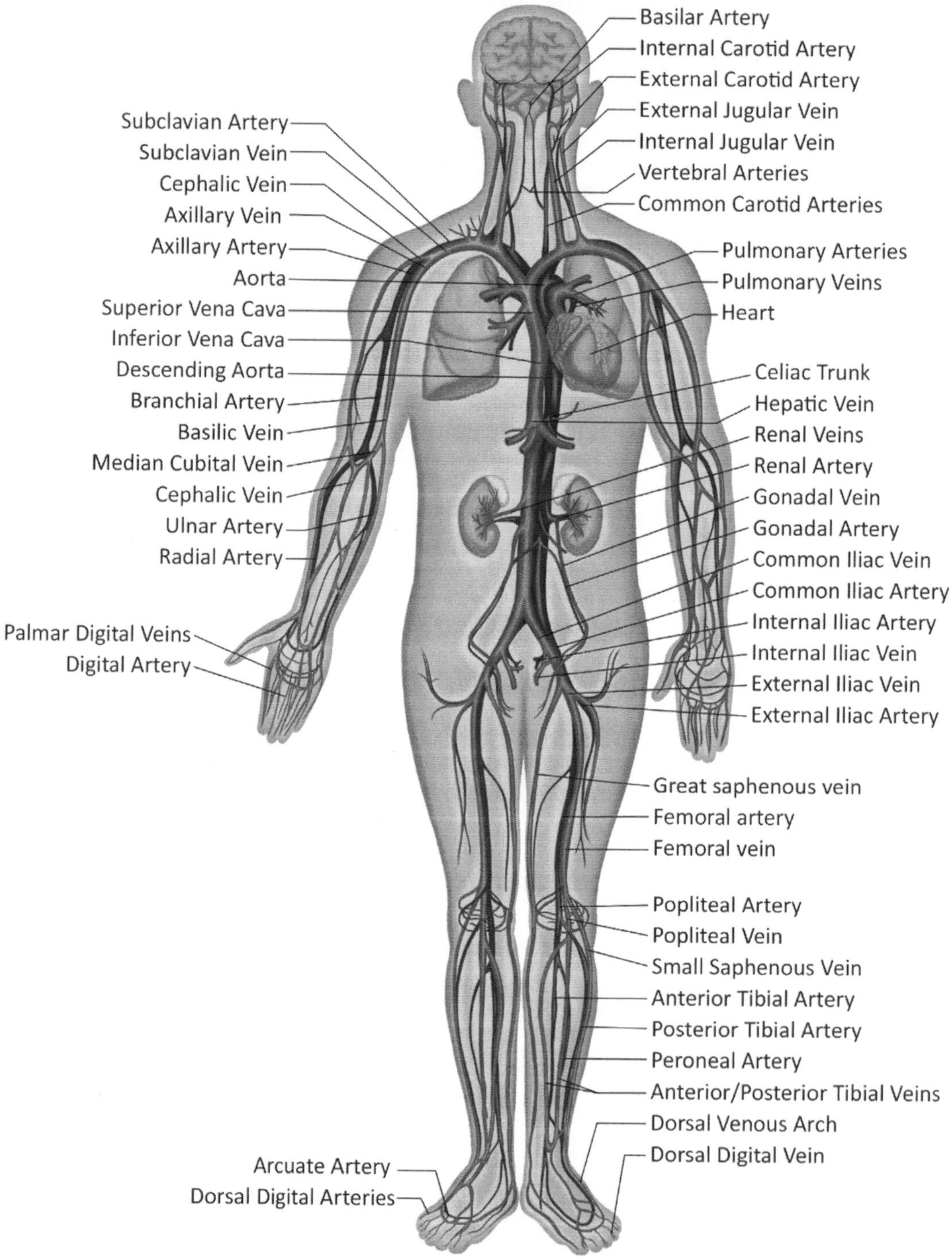

The Heart

The superior vena cava collects blood from the upper half of the body, while the inferior vena cava collects blood from the lower half of the body. The superior and inferior vena cava take oxygen-deficient blood to the right atrium. The tricuspid valve pushes blood into the right ventricle. From the right ventricle, it moves through the pulmonary valve and travels through the pulmonary artery to the lungs to become oxygen enriched. Once the blood has become oxygen-rich, it returns to the left atrium via the pulmonary vein. The left atrium contracts and pushes the blood through the mitral valve into the left ventricle. Blood is through the aortic valve into the aorta when the ventricle contracts. Blood travels to the rest of the body from the aorta. Blood flows away from the heart in arteries, which branch into arterioles, and then into capillaries. Blood returns to the heart in veins.

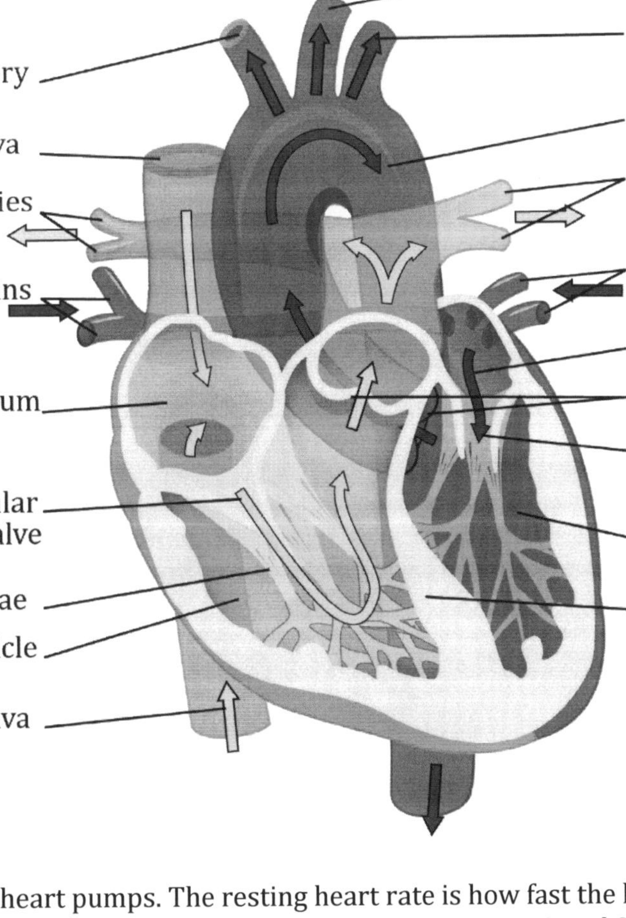

Heart rate is how fast the heart pumps. The resting heart rate is how fast the heart beats when the body is at rest. The average adult has a resting heart rate of between 70 and 80 beats every minute.

Stroke volume refers to much blood the heart pumps out with each beat. The average adult has a stroke volume of between 75 and 80 milliliters per beat. Stroke volume is a more complex measurement than heart rate.

Cardiac output is a measure of the heart's performance. To determine cardiac output, multiply the stroke volume by the heart rate.

Respiratory System

The respiratory (pulmonary) system brings oxygen to the entire body. Inhalation occurs through the nose and mouth. The warm, moist environment of the nose and mouth warms the air. The air then travels to the lungs through the bronchial tubes; while in the lungs, cilia trap foreign particles and germs and remove them through sneezing or coughing. Carbon dioxide exits the body through exhalation. The body remains in homeostasis throughout the process.

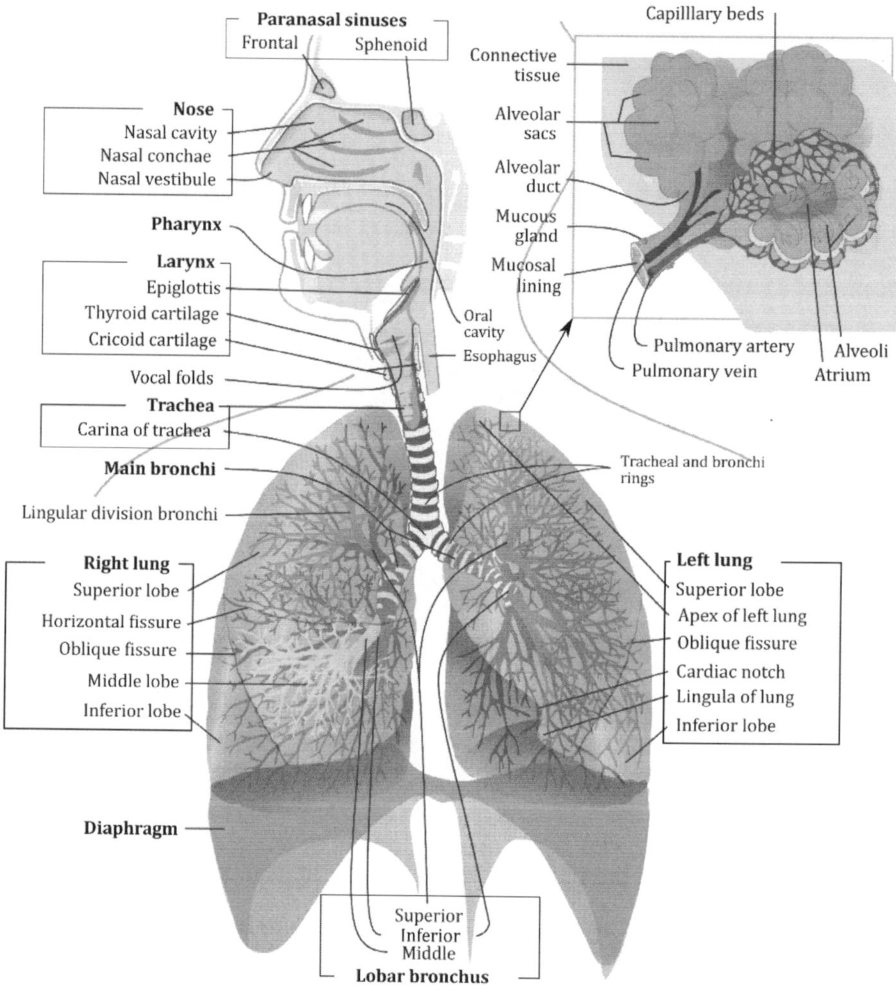

Human respiration is a four-step process involving breathing, external respiration, internal respiration, and cellular respiration. Breathing is the process of bringing oxygen into the lungs. External respiration occurs when oxygen replaces carbon dioxide within the alveoli. Internal respiration removes excess carbon dioxide from the lungs. Cellular respiration, involves oxygen breaking down sugar within the cells to produce water, ATP, energy, and carbon dioxide.

Breathing is the process of inhaling oxygen (inspiration) and exhaling its waste product, carbon dioxide (exhalation). Inspiration requires the muscles to work while exhalation is an involuntary, reflexive action.

The respiratory pump is the entire respiratory physiology, located in the chest and body. It includes hard and soft tissues (bones such as the sternum and ribs) and muscles such as the diaphragm and the sternocleidomastoid.

Review Video: Respiratory System
Visit mometrix.com/academy and enter code: 783075

Respiratory Process

The respiratory process operates in the following order:

1. Oxygen is inhaled through the nose and mouth and down the trachea.
2. The oxygen passes into the bronchi.
3. The oxygen fills the lungs and alveoli.
4. The blood is pumped into the heart.
5. The blood is pumped into the lungs.
6. The blood is infused with oxygen.
7. The oxygenated blood is pumped back into the heart.
8. The oxygenated blood is pumped throughout the body.

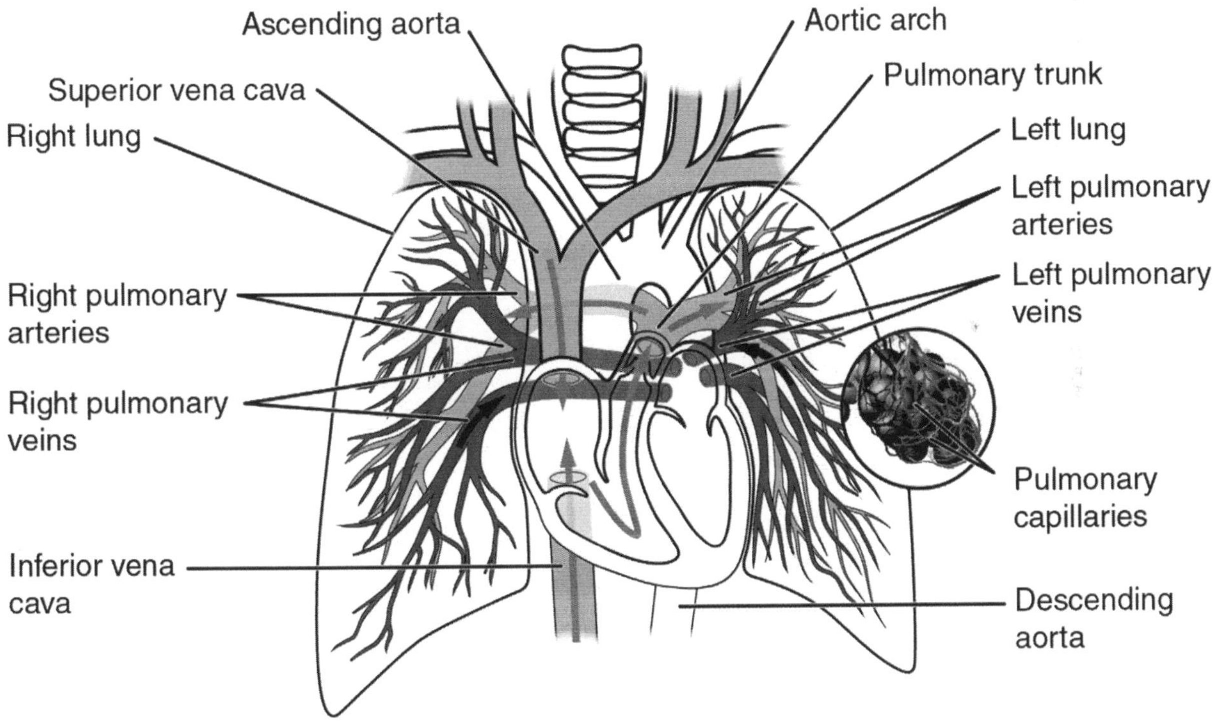

Heart Rate and Blood Pressure During Exercise

During exercise, heart rate increases linearly along with the increase in intensity. Heart rate is also affected by age, body position (sitting, standing, lying), fitness ability, activity type, presence of heart disease, medications, blood volume, and environmental factors (heat, humidity, cold). Systolic blood pressure behaves in a similar manner and increases linearly with the exercise workload. Diastolic blood pressure may decrease slightly or remain unchanged throughout the duration because there is a decrease in peripheral resistance so that the working muscles may receive the blood, and thus oxygen, which they need.

Effect of Breathing on Exercise

Breathing allows the body to absorb oxygen through the alveoli and clear the carbon dioxide from the system. It is important that the client not hyperventilate (breathe too quickly) during the exercise session. When this happens, there is not sufficient time to clear the carbon dioxide from the body during respiratory processes, and fatigue quickly ensues, leading to a premature ending of the exercise session. The Valsalva maneuver (holding one's breath while straining) is also detrimental to exercise because holding one's breath causes an unnatural rise in heart rate and blood pressure and can lead to extreme discomfort, fainting, or dizziness. It is the personal trainer's job to remind the client to breathe at the appropriate times.

Directions of Body Movement

Anatomic Reference Points:

- Proximal (nearest to the body center, joint center, or reference point)
- Distal (away from the body center, joint center, or reference point)
- Superior (above, toward the head)
- Inferior (lower than, toward the feet)
- Anterior (ventral) (toward the front)
- Posterior (dorsal) (toward the back)
- Medial (closer to the midline)
- Lateral (away from the midline)

Movement Types:

- pronation (rolling inward)
- supination (rolling outward)
- flexion (movement that decreases the joint angle)
- extension (movement that increases the joint angle)
- hyperextension (movement that increases the joint angle unnaturally)
- adduction (movement toward the midline of the body)
- abduction (movement away from the midline of the body)
- rotation (movement to the right or left, usually of the head and neck)
- circumduction (compound circular movement including flexion, extension, abduction, adduction)
- plantarflexion (extension at the ankle joint)
- dorsiflexion (flexion at the ankle joint)

Muscle Classification:

- agonist (initiates movement)
- antagonist (opposes the agonist muscle action)
- Synergist (assists the prime mover but is not the primary muscle responsible for the action)
- Stabilizer (contracts to hold one body part immobile so another body part can be mobile)

Relation of Directions and Planes of Movement to Resistance Exercise

Understanding the directions to describe exercises is essential to putting together a well-rounded exercise routine. It also allows the personal trainer to assess full range of motion for joints and give proper instruction to the client during each session. The trainer is provided a limitless array of modifications and ways to make the workout more challenging for the client as needed simply by changing the direction of the movement. It also allows the trainer to observe abnormal patterns of movement that exist in the client and that can be fixed.

Planes of Movement

The planes of movement are as follows: frontal/coronal (divides the body into front and back sections), sagittal (divides the body into right and left sections), midsagittal (divides the body into equal right and left sections), and transverse (divides the body into top and bottom sections). Understanding the different planes of movement allows the personal trainer to create effective exercise routines that work each section of the body independently or in conjunction with the others. It allows for assessment of weaker muscle groups and allows for increased flexibility through all planes of movement.

Plane	Description
Coronal (frontal)	Divides the body into front and back sections
Sagittal	Divides the body into right and left sections
Midsagittal	Divides the body into equal right and left sections
Transverse (horizontal)	Divides the body into top and bottom sections

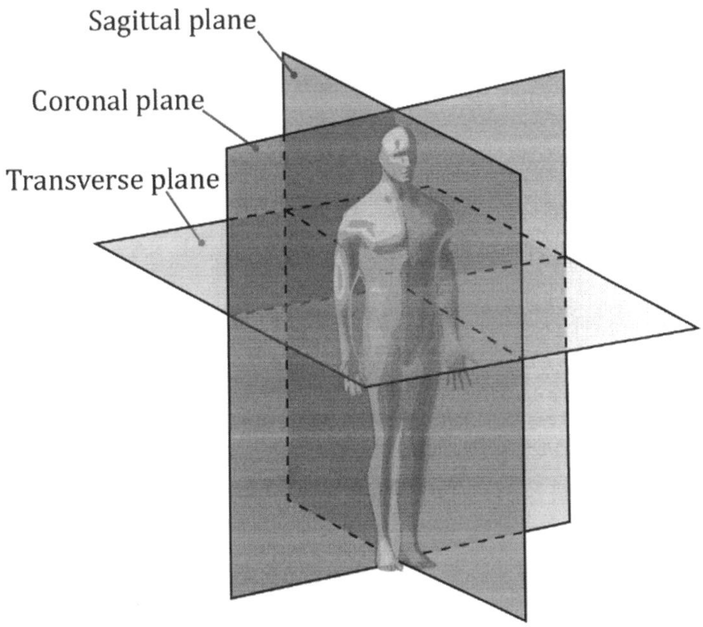

Spine

The human spine contains 33 vertebrae divided into 5 sections: cervical (7 bones), thoracic (12 bones), lumbar (5 bones), sacral (5 bones fused into the sacrum), and the coccygeal (4 bones fused into the coccyx).The spine can move through all planes of movement (frontal, sagittal, midsagittal, and transverse) by bending forward (flexion), bending backward (extension), bnding to the side (side flexion), and twisting (rotation). Some common ailments of the spine include lower back pain, bulging disc (vertebral disc bulges outward), and herniated disc (tear in the wall of the disc). Lower back pain is common among clients and can often be due to increased weight gain in the midsection. If disc problems are present, it is important to have these properly diagnosed by medical personnel and to modify the exercise sessions accordingly. Some twisting movements may need to be avoided, and clients may need to spend most of their time using machine weights where they are properly supported. High-impact activities should be avoided.

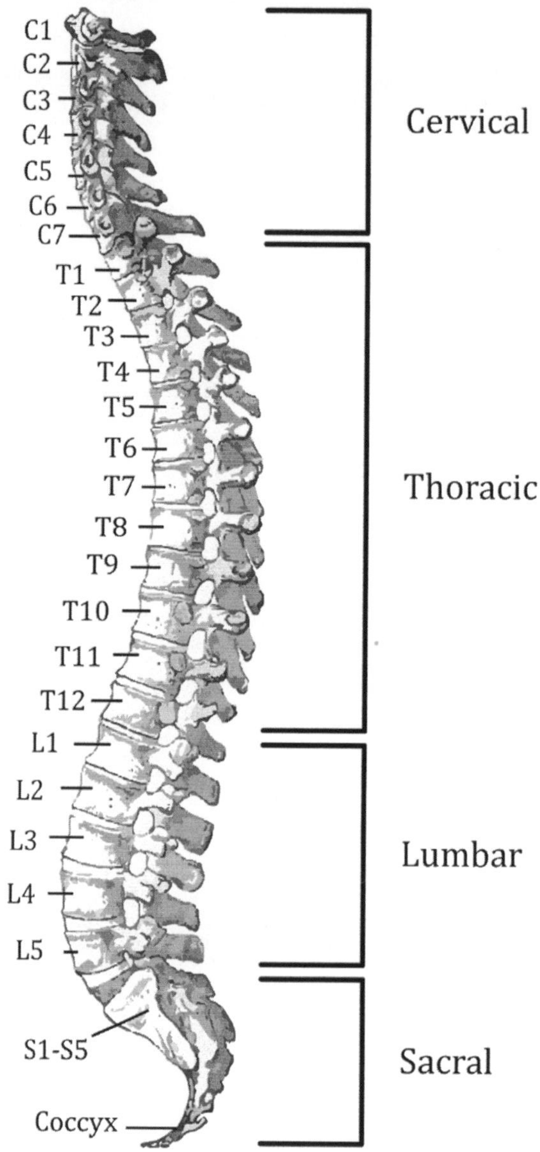

Irregular Curves

Lordosis is the excessive curvature of the lumbar spine, kyphosis is the excessive curvature of the thoracic spine (i.e., hunchback appearance), and scoliosis is a lateral S-shaped curve of the spine. If a client displays an abnormal curvature, they should avoid performing movements that put excessive stress on the spine. For example, stable, closed kinetic chain movements are more helpful than open kinetic chain movements. Lordosis can cause discomfort in the lumbar spine and make many high-impact exercises uncomfortable; standing for long periods of time can also be painful. Scoliosis and kyphosis can cause difficulty in completing full range of motion, and certain exercises may need to be off limits for the client. It is not advisable to engage in high impact activities or activities that require excessive torsion (twisting of the spine) if the client has a spinal condition. It is advisable to utilize machine weights to provide proper support for clients with extreme cases of lordosis, kyphosis, and scoliosis. In addition, it may be necessary as to avoid high-impact activities.

Aerobic and Anaerobic Energy Systems

The anaerobic pathway uses the ATP-PC (Phosphagen) system and glycolysis to generate ATP. The ATP-PC system uses stored ATP in the muscles. There is a limited supply of ATP in the muscles, and this system can only fuel 5 seconds of activity. After ATP reserves are consumed, the PC system can provide fuel for an additional 25 seconds of energy. Glycolysis (Nonoxidative System) uses carbohydrates to create ATP by partially breaking down glucose and does not need oxygen to complete the process; lactic acid is its byproduct. Glycolysis provides sufficient energy to sustain 30 seconds to 3 minutes of activity before aerobic energy pathways take over. The body stores carbohydrates as glycogen in the muscles. Glycogen is converted to glucose during glycolysis. The aerobic pathway (Oxidative System) uses oxygen to break down carbohydrates, proteins, and fats to create usable energy for the body and is used to fuel endurance activities lasting longer than 3 minutes. As heart rate climbs and ventilation increases after the first few minutes of an exercise session, plenty of oxygen becomes available in the bloodstream to convert glucose to ATP. If there is insufficient oxygen to fuel the muscles, the nonoxidative system has to support the process, resulting in a build up of lactic acid. The process is referred to as the lactic threshold.

The primary fuel source for aerobic metabolism is oxygen. Anaerobic metabolism does not require oxygen. The ATP-PC system and glycolysis create usable energy during anaerobic metabolism. A walk or light jog are examples of light aerobic activity. An example of an anaerobic activity is explosive powerlifting or plyometrics.

ATP Formation

ATP stands for adenosine triphosphate. The energy found in ATP comes from a process called hydrolysis. The enzyme ATP-ase separates a phosphate ion from the ATP, creating usable energy during hydrolysis. ATP becomes ADP (adenosine diphosphate) since it only has two phosphate ions attached. Food is the fuel source consumed during ADP to create more ATP formation.

Glycolysis

Glycolysis converts glucose into pyruvate, with two net ATP and two NADH as byproducts. The process of glycolysis occurs during aerobic and anaerobic activities. Pyruvate then enters into the Krebs cycle, where it will produce an additional two ATP. The process of glycolysis does not require oxygen (anaerobic) and does not result in substantial energy production.

Krebs Cycle

The Krebs cycle is also called the citric acid cycle or the tricarboxylic acid cycle (TCA). It is a catabolic pathway in which the bonds of glucose and occasionally fats or lipids are broken down and reformed into ATP. It is a respiration process that uses oxygen and produces carbon dioxide, water, and ATP. Cells require energy from ATP to synthesize proteins from amino acids and replicate DNA. One of the products of the Krebs cycle is NADH, which is then used in the electron chain transport system to manufacture ATP. From glycolysis, pyruvate is oxidized in a step linking to the Krebs cycle. After the Krebs cycle, NADH and succinate are oxidized in the electron transport chain.

Normal Acute Response to Cardiovascular and Resistance Training

The normal, immediate response to cardiovascular exercises is for heart rate, blood pressure, and ventilation to increase. This increase transitions the body from anaerobic to aerobic energy pathways by filling the body with oxygen that can be converted to energy. As the body adapts to cardiovascular training, measurable changes to the body's heart rate occur. Resting heart rate lowers and the client requires increased intensity to bring the heart rate to the ideal training zone during an exercise session. The normal, immediate response to resistance exercise is for heart rate and blood pressure to increase, but they do not stay elevated (unlike the cardiovascular response).

Normal Chronic Response to Cardiovascular and Resistance Training

The chronic response to cardiovascular training lowers resting blood pressure and heart rate. In addition, it takes more intensity to increase heart rate and blood pressure, so the client can exercise for longer durations or higher intensities. Lactic acid is cleared from the muscles more effectively, and in longer endurance sessions (e.g., marathons, etc.) can be converted to usable energy. Repetitive resistance training helps to condition the anaerobic system and also can increase the size of the muscle fibers. Depending upon the mode used in resistance training, strength, power, or muscle definition can be increased. Over time, the client can experience positive benefits such as weight loss, increased coordination, increased strength, and increased motivation for exercise.

Warm-Up and Cooldown

The warm-up helps prepare the body for exercise by slightly increasing heart and blood pressure to move blood to the working muscles. The warm-up should move from general (which prepares the cardiovascular system) to specific (which targets specific muscles). A complete warm-up prevents injury, increases flexibility, and improves joint range of motion. A proper cool down helps to lower the heart rate to resting levels safely; skipping the cool down can lead to dysrhythmias because of a slight decrease in venous return. The warm-up and cool down are integral parts of an exercise routine and should not be ignored. They promote safety in training, increase range of motion and flexibility, and prepare the body to enter and exit the training session.

Overtraining

It is normal for a client to experience fatigue for a few days after training; sharp or persistent pain (lasting longer than one week) can be an indication of injury or overtraining. Possible signs and symptoms of overtraining include: fatigue, feelings of moodiness and irritation, depression, lack of enthusiasm about future workouts, and sleep problems. In addition, a client may notice an abnormally elevated heart rate during cardiovascular exercise, a decrease in overall performance, and lowered immunity to sickness. Overtraining may not occur under the personal trainer's supervision, but when the client trains independently. It is important, therefore, to be aware of all the aspects of a client's training program.

Physiological Adaptations During Continued Exercise at Submaximal Levels

Continued submaximal exercise can produce positive effects in the nervous system, muscular system, and skeletal system. The nervous system responds quickly to training, and motor units in the spine begin to activate faster and more often, becoming more efficient in stimulating muscle fibers to begin working and adapting to exercise. Training results in strength and power gains. The muscle fibers begin to grow and increase in number as a response to continued resistance training. Bone density begins to increase, which is particularly helpful for women as they age. Within the cardiovascular system, the heart becomes more effective at pumping blood, resting heart rate and blood pressure are lowered, and the number of capillaries increases to allow better perfusion of oxygen and carbon dioxide. Continued resistance training also increases mitochondrial and capillary density in the muscles and more effectively uses oxygen for energy. Maximal exercise should be reserved for testing, as it does not provide additional benefit but increases injury risk.

Rest as Part of the Training Cycle

Adequate rest between training sessions is an integral part of the training cycle. It allows the bodily systems to recover from the stress of exercise and to prepare for the next session. Without adequate rest, the client will find it more difficult to lose weight, increase performance, and be motivated for workouts. Inadequate rest will lead to overtraining and possible injury. It is up to the personal trainer to explain the importance of rest to the client because the initial reaction is to exercise more often or longer than necessary, hoping to achieve results in less time. Particularly if the client has a history of being sedentary, he may hope to make up for any "lost" time.

Differences in Training for Muscular Strength and Endurance

Increased repetitions and decreased weight improve muscular endurance and decreased repetitions and increased weight improve muscular strength. The goals set by the client during pre-exercise screening and fitness testing determine whether the program is designed to achieve muscular strength or endurance. Most often, an increase in muscular strength is the area that needs attention first so the client can successfully complete activities of daily living.

Changes in Blood Pressure

When moving from a standing to a sitting or a lying position, blood pressure and heart rate decrease. When moving from a lying position to a sitting or standing position, blood pressure and heart rate increase. When sitting or lying down, gravity acts on the splanchnic region to lower aortic pressure and thus blood pressure and heart rate. Blood pressure at rest can remain low through continued exercise as the arteries and veins become more pliable, and blood can flow through with less effort.

Isotonic/Isometric and Concentric/Eccentric Muscle Contractions

An isometric contraction occurs when the muscle contracts but does not change shape, whereas an isotonic contraction occurs when the muscle contracts and shortens to overcome the weight of a specific load. The isotonic contraction occurs in two phases: the eccentric (lengthening) phase and the concentric (shortening) phase. An example of an isometric exercise would be performing a plank because there is tension in the muscles but they are not shortening or lengthening. An example of an isotonic exercise would be a push-up because various muscles are shortening or lengthening to complete the movement.

Contraction Type	Result
Isometric	No change in length
Isotonic (eccentric)	Muscle lengthens
Isotonic (concentric)	Muscle shortens

MAJOR MUSCLE GROUPS

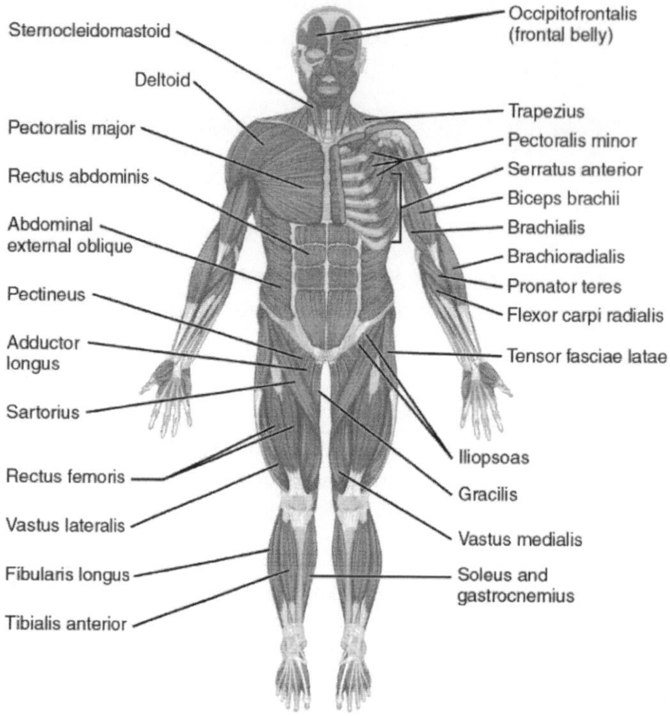

Major muscles of the body. Right side: superficial; left side: deep (anterior view)

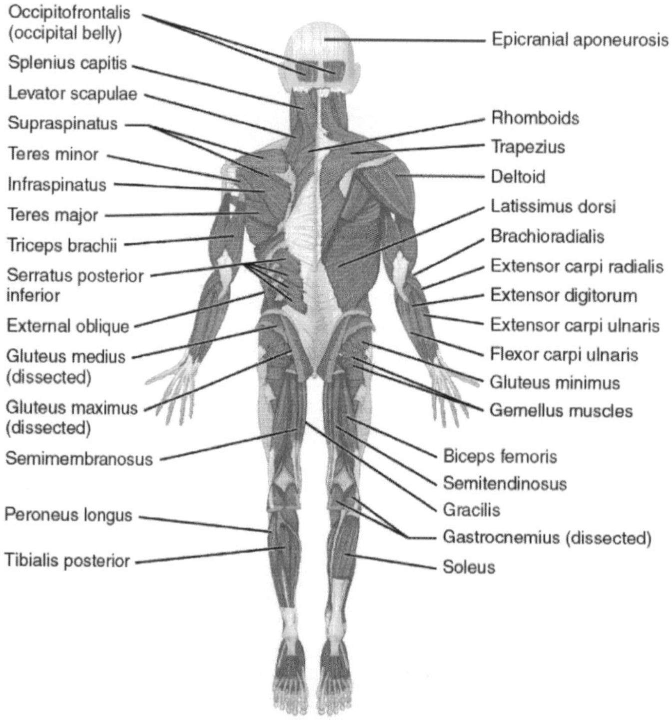

Major muscles of the body. Right side: superficial; left side: deep (posterior view)

Lower Leg Complex

Anterior tibialis—runs along the outside of the tibia from under the knee to the ankle. It helps stabilize the foot.

Posterior tibialis—runs along the back of the tibia, under the fibula. It helps control the foot.

Soleus—the fleshy part of the back of the lower leg. It also runs down the sides of the Achilles' tendon. It controls walking motion in the leg and ankle and supports the foot.

Gastrocnemius—on the back of the leg below the knee. It works with the soleus to control walking and stabilize the foot.

Peroneus longus—runs along the tibia on the outer part of the leg. It flexes and everts the foot.

Hamstring Complex

Biceps femoris (long head)—emanates from the pelvis and inserts at the top of the fibula. It is essential in knee and hip movement.

Biceps femoris (short head)—runs along the lower part of the back of the femur. It is essential to knee and tibia movement.

Semimembranosus—runs along the back femur, through the center of the leg. It is essential to hip, knee, and tibia movement.

Semitendinosus—runs along the back of the femur toward the inner thigh. It is essential to hip, knee, and tibia movement.

Quadriceps Complex

Vastus lateralis—runs along the outside of the front thigh. It stabilizes the knee and controls all movement for that joint.

Vastus medialis—runs along the inner thigh close to the knee. It is essential to all movement for the knee joint.

Vastus intermedius—runs along the vastus lateralis, the length of the front thigh. It is also essential to all movement for the knee joint.

Rectus femoris—runs down the center of the front thigh. It is also essential to knee motion and stability.

Hip Musculature Complex

Adductor longus, adductor magnus (anterior fibers), adductor magnus (posterior fibers), and adductor brevis—fall under the pelvis, interwoven at the top of the femur. Together, they control hip adduction, abduction, flexion, and rotation.

Gracilis—runs along the interior of the top of the femur. It is also essential to all elements of hip movement.

Pectineus—runs along the back edge of the upper part of the femur. It is also essential to all elements of hip movement.

Gluteus medius (anterior fibers), gluteus medius (posterior fibers), gluteus minimus—run along the outer edge of the back of the pelvis. Together, they control hip adduction, abduction, flexion, and rotation.

Tensor fascia lata (TFL)—runs along the top of the outer part of the hip. It is essential to hip flexion, abduction, adduction, and rotation.

Gluteus maximus—the fleshy part of the buttocks. It affects hip rotation and extension as well as stabilizing the lumbo-pelvic-hip (LPH) complex.

Psoas—run along the top of the hips to the base of the lowest vertebrae. These muscles are essential to hip movement and the rotation of the lumbar spine.

Iliacus —runs along the iliac crest. These muscles are essential to hip movement and lumbo-pelvic stability.

Sartorius—runs across the top of the thigh from the outer hip to the inner thigh. This muscle affects hip and knee function.

Piriformis—rests along the front of the sacrum. It affects hip movement stabilizes the hip joint.

Abdominal Musculature

Rectus abdominis—run along the midline of the abdomen. They affect and control all core motion.

External oblique—run down the sides of the torso. They affect and control all core motion.

Internal oblique—run under the external obliques along the sides of the torso. They affect and control all core motion as well as stabilize the lumbo-pelvic-hip (LPH) complex.

Transversus abdominis—run along the side of the torso up and across under the ribs. They help stabilize the internal organs and the LPH complex.

Diaphragm—runs underneath the rib cage. It pulls open the thoracic cavity to accommodate oxygen intake.

Muscles of the Back

Superficial erector spinae—the following muscles run down the length of the spine. Together they control spinal movement and stabilize the spine during activity:

- Iliocostalis
- Longissimus
- Spinalis

Latissimus dorsi—runs across the back under the scapula. It is critical to shoulder movement.

Quadratus lumborum—runs along the lower back and connects to the top of the pelvis. It affects spinal flexion and also stabilizes the lumbo-pelvic-hip (LPH) complex.

Transversospinalis Complex

Semispinalis —the following muscles run from the bottom of the back of the skull to the top of the shoulders and spine. Together they control the movement of the upper spine as well as the head:

- Iliocostalis
- Longissmus
- Spinalis

Multifidus—run along the spine down into the sacrum. They control spinal flexion and lower-hip rotation.

Muscles in the Shoulder

Serratus anterior—runs around the rib cage underneath the armpit. They affect the movement of the scapula.

Rhomboids—run across the top middle of the back, just under the neck. They also affect the movement of the scapula.

Lower trapezius, middle trapezius, and upper trapezius—run along the sides of the spine from the base of the neck down. They are also essential to all aspects of movement of the scapula.

Pectoralis major—runs along the front of the chest. It is essential to all movement of the shoulder complex.

Pectoralis minor—connects the front of the shoulder to the top ribs. It pulls the scapula forward.

Deltoid—the fleshy muscle that runs along the top of the arm. It is essential to all shoulder movement.

Teres major—runs along the chest to under the armpit. It is essential to shoulder rotation and movement.

Muscles in the Arm

Biceps brachii—runs along the top length of the humerus. It is essential to shoulder and elbow movement.

Triceps—runs along the bottom of the humerus (the back of the upper arm). It supports shoulder and elbow movement.

Brachioradialis—runs along the outside of the humerus (the side of the upper arm). It supports elbow movement.

Brachialis—runs along the outside of the humerus (the side of the upper arm). It supports elbow movement.

Rotator Cuff Muscles

Teres minor—runs along the lateral edge of the scapula. It accelerates and decelerates shoulder rotation.

Infraspinatus—sits under and along the scapula. It accelerates and decelerates shoulder rotation.

Subscapularis—covers the back along the scapula. It accelerates and decelerates shoulder rotation.

Supraspinatus—runs along the interior of the top of the shoulder. It helps accelerate abduction and decelerate adduction of the arm.

Muscles in the Neck

Sternocleidomastoid—runs from the side of the back of the head down to the cervical collar. They help control the movement of the head and cervical spine.

Scalenes—run down the sides of the neck at the shoulders. They help stabilize and control the movement of the cervical spine.

Longus coli—run along the sides of the cervical vertebrae. They help control the movement of the cervical spine.

Longus capitis—runs along the side of the neck. It helps stabilize and move the cervical spine.

Levator scapulae—runs along the side of the neck down to the top of the shoulder. It affects the up/down motion of the scapula.

Major Bones

The major bones of the body include the following:

- skull
- cervical vertebrae
- thoracic vertebrae
- lumbar vertebrae
- pectoral girdle
- sternum
- ribs
- humerus
- radius
- ulna
- carpus
- metacarpals
- phalanges (hands)
- hip bones and sacrum
- coccyx
- pubic symphysis
- femur
- patella
- tibia
- fibula
- tarsus
- metatarsals
- phalanges (feet)

It is important for the personal trainer to understand the major bones in the skeletal system so they can be used as reference points to properly inform and educate a client on what exercise is working.

Joint Classifications

There are six types of joint classifications: hinge (flexion/extension; knee), pivot (rotation of one bone around another; neck), ball and socket joint (flexion/extension, external/internal rotation, adduction/abduction; hip), saddle joint (flexion/extension, adduction/abduction, circumduction; thumb), condylar or ellipsoidal joint (flexion/extension, no rotation; joints between metacarpals and phalanges), plane or gliding joint (connection of flat bone joints; clavicular joints).

Joint Classification	Function	Example
Hinge	Flexion/extension	Knee
Pivot	Rotation of one bound around another	Neck
Ball and Socket	flexion/extension, external/internal rotation, adduction/abduction	Hip
Saddle	flexion/extension, adduction/abduction, circumduction	Thumb
Condylar or Ellipsoidal	Flexion/extension, no rotation	Joints between metacarpals and phalanges
Plane or Gliding	Connection of flat bone joints	Clavicular joints

Agonist/Antagonist Muscle Movements

Muscles do not work in isolation, and joint movement involves muscle synergies. The agonist muscle initiates movement, while the antagonist muscle opposes that movement. For instance, in a bicep curl, the biceps brachii is the agonist muscle that initiates the eccentric part of the curl, and the triceps brachii acts as the antagonist muscle. When doing resistance exercises, it is very important to work within the accepted range of motion; hyperextending joints or muscles will increase injury and could cause misalignment of the bones through repetitive hyperextension. If a client injures himself early in the training regimen, it could negatively affect his motivation and faithfulness to exercise.

A force-couple refers to two forces acting simultaneously on an object with equal force in the opposite direction; for example, pedaling a bike or working an arm ergometer. Force-couples can also exist inside the body when opposing forces act upon bones. One example would be moving the arm backward in the horizontal plane. The agonist and antagonist muscles are exerting force to pull and push the arm backward.

Muscle Length-Tension Relationship

The length of a muscle at rest and the amount of tension the muscle can produce at rest is referred to as the length-tension relationship. The optimal muscle length occurs when the actin and myosin have the greatest degree of overlap. Optimal muscle length results in maximal force production. Increasing the length of a muscle reduces force production because actin and myosin overlap is limited. Shortening a muscle causes excessive overlap of actin and myosin, which limits force production. When the length-tension relationship is altered, the entire HMS is adversely affected.

Reciprocal Inhibition

Reciprocal inhibition occurs when the muscles on one side of a joint relax while the muscles on the other side of the joint contract. Reciprocal inhibition helps to create coordinated movement during exercise. During a bicep curl, for instance, reciprocal inhibition is the way in which the biceps contract while the triceps lengthen.

Synergistic Dominance

Synergistic dominance occurs when the secondary mover initiates muscle action in place of the prime mover. Synergistic dominance can occur because of an injured prime mover, an underdeveloped prime mover, or an overdeveloped secondary mover (synergist). An injury is likely once the synergist dominates because it was not designed to handle the load appropriately.

Hypertrophy, Atrophy, and Hyperplasia

Hypertrophy of a muscle refers to an increase in the size of the muscle fibers. In turn, this increases client strength which can positively impact her activities of daily living. Atrophy occurs when a muscle group is not worked effectively or often and refers to a decrease in the size of the muscle fibers. Atrophy decreases strength and ability to perform normal tasks. Atrophy can be a result of overlooking the training of a particular muscle group or can be the result of an accident. Hyperplasia refers to an increase in the number of muscle fibers. Resistance training can be used to overcome atrophy and increase hypertrophy of the muscle fibers. Hyperplasia has not been well documented in humans; however, with proper resistance training and rest periods, muscles can recover more quickly from the micro-tears that are a result of continued training.

Cardiovascular Fitness, Muscular Strength, Endurance, and Body Composition

Cardiovascular fitness creates a healthy heart by lowering resting blood pressure and heart rate and increasing the elasticity of arteries and veins. Muscular strength and endurance help clients perform activities of daily living with ease and crosses paths with cardiovascular fitness in that both areas can be used to prevent disease or reduce its symptoms. Cardiovascular fitness and muscular strength and endurance training also help reduce body composition, which in turn lowers the risk of disease for the client. It is the best option for the client to work within all areas of fitness to achieve the best results.

Components of Fitness

There are at least four components of fitness that help an individual become well-rounded in his training:

- body composition (a measure of the ratio of fat, muscle, bone, and water in the human body)
- muscular endurance (the muscles capacity to continuously and repeatedly produce force)
- muscular strength (a measure of how much force the muscle can produce)
- aerobic capacity (measures the amount of work that can be performed, typically defined in terms of oxygen consumption and it).

These components should be measured on a semi-regular basis, and one should not be emphasized over the others; the exception is when one area is significantly weaker than the others.

Fitness Component	What it Measures	Measurement Example
Body composition	a measure of the ratio of fat, muscle, bone, and water in the human body	BMI, circumfernce measurements,
Muscular endurance	the muscles capacity to continuously and repeatedly produce force	Maximum number of repetitions that can be formed of a single exercise
Muscular strength	a measure of how much force the muscle can produce	Maximum amount of weight that can be lifted in a single repetition
Aerobic capacity	measures the amount of work that can be performed, typically defined in terms of oxygen consumption and it	One mile run

Contraindications to Exercise Testing

If a client experiences any of the following issues, she should not undergo exercise testing:

- an EKG reading that indicates a recent acute cardiac event or ischemia
- unstable angina
- uncontrolled dysrhythmia of the heart that has other symptoms present
- severe aortic stenosis
- uncontrolled heart failure with accompanying symptoms
- acute myo- or pericarditis
- history of aneurysm or suspicion that patient might have an aneurysm
- Any acute infection where fever, body aches, or swollen lymph nodes are observed

For these clients, the risk posed by exercise testing outweighs any benefits.

If a client experiences any of the following issues, she may still go through the exercise testing process as long as the benefits of the testing will outweigh the risks involved:

- left main coronary stenosis
- moderate stenotic valvular heart disease
- abnormalities in electrolyte balance
- severe hypertension (systolic BP of >200 mmHg and/or diastolic BP of >110 mmHg)
- tachydysrhythmia or bradydysrhythmia
- hypertrophic cardiomyopathy (any other forms of outflow tract obstruction)
- neuromuscular/musculoskeletal/ rheumatoid disorders that will be aggravated by exercise
- high-degree AV block
- ventricular aneurysm
- uncontrolled metabolic disease
- chronic infectious disease
- Mental or physical impairment that leads to an inability to exercise properly

Laboratory Testing Procedures for Body Fat Analysis

There are several viable procedures for assessing body fat. Skinfold measurements, circumference measurements, and body mass index are often used because they are easily accessible in the field by personal trainers and other allied health professionals. Skinfold measurements pinch specific sites on the skin with calipers to measure subcutaneous body fat. To promote consistency when measuring skin folds, take all measurements on the right side of the body. The four measurement locations are:

- a vertical fold of skin on the anterior side of the biceps, halfway between the elbow and shoulder
- a vertical fold of skin on the posterior side of the triceps, halfway between the elbow and shoulder
- an angled fold of skin (about 45 degrees) at the subscapula, about two centimeters below the inner angle of the scapula
- and an angled fold of skin (of about 45 degrees) just above the iliac crest and in line with the apex of the armpit

The Durnin-Womersly chart or formula provides the client's body fat percentage based on the sum of the four caliper measurements, the client's age, and the client's gender. Circumference measurements assess different body sites with a measuring strip; the measurements are then added together. ACSM recommends measuring the abdomen, calf, forearm, hips, upper arm, waist, and thigh. All measurements should be taken from the anatomical position on the right side of the body. The body mass index takes different factors (age, weight, height), puts them in an equation, and gets an approximation of body fat percentage. BMI is calculated by dividing body weight in kilograms by height in meters squared (kg·m-2). Of these three field calculations, the skinfold measurements provide the most accurate body fat percentage; however, when dealing with clients who are sensitive about their weight or are extremely obese, girth measurements or BMI might be more helpful, even if it is not as accurate. The drawback for BMI is that it can't distinguish between fat and fat-free mass; a muscular person and an obese person could have a similar BMI. In the laboratory, more accurate methods can be used such as BOD POD (uses air displacement to measure body fat and is most accurate), bioelectrical impedance (measures resistance to electrical flow through the body to determine fat and fat-free mass), infrared (uses an infrared light to determine fat and fat-free mass), and DEXA (measures bone mineral density). These methods, however, are expensive and not able to be used in the field very easily.

Predicted Body Fat Percentage

Gender	BMI (kg/m^2)	20–39 years	40–59 years	60–79 years
Men	<18.5	<8%	<11%	<13%
	18.6-24.9	8%–19%	11%–21%	13%–24%
	25.0–29.9	20%–24%	22%–27%	25%–29%
	>30	≥25%	≥28%	≥30%
Women	<18.5	<21%	<23%	<24%
	18.6-24.9	21%–32%	23%–33%	24%–35%
	25.0–29.9	33%–38%	34%–39%	36%–41%
	>30	≥39%	≥40%	≥42%

Exercise Tests

The following tests can be used easily in the field: body composition (skinfold or circumference measurements), cardiovascular fitness (1.5-mile run test), muscular strength (1 RM or multiple RM test), muscular endurance (push-up test), and flexibility (sit and reach). Tests should be performed so that the energy system responsible for that test is not completely taxed before the test. Additionally, adequate rest should be taken in between each test.

Field Tests vs. Laboratory Tests of Body Fat Analysis

Field tests and laboratory tests for body fat assessment vary significantly. Field tests require minimal equipment and are simple to perform with a client. Laboratory tests are more accurate but require expensive equipment to carry out and are not necessary for every client. Very few clients need the specificity of laboratory equipment. Exercise science studies need that exactitude in calculations. A personal trainer needs enough information to set accurate goals for the client to achieve health benefits and field body fat tests are able to provide that.

Appropriate Fitness Assessments for Special Conditions and Injuries

After processing the paperwork, administer the fitness assessment. Note special conditions or injuries prior to exercise testing. Make sure to select a fitness test that is appropriate for the client's health and physical ability. For instance, if the client is overweight or out of shape, the running test may not be appropriate, but the 6-minute walk test is suitable. If the client has a shoulder injury, the push-up test would not be appropriate, but the abdominal curl-ups would work. To have a well-rounded view of the client's overall health, the personal trainer should assess all five areas of fitness without aggravating an injury. If the client has limitations, modify the assessments appropriately.

Order of Fitness Assessments

When the client arrives, conduct a body fat analysis as it is minimally invasive and does not tax the client physically. The exercise screening should follow. When conducting the exercise screening, start with cardiovascular tests because they use the largest muscle groups. Performing other tests prior to cardiovascular testing causes undue fatigue. Muscular fitness assessments should come next. When determining what weight to use for the one-repetition maximum (1-RM) tests, be sure to give 3–5 minutes of rest between each of the submaximal 1-RM warm-up repetitions. Flexibility tests are the final component of fitness testing because the muscles have had time to warm up, which minimizes injury risk.

Interpretation and Explanation of Test Results

Compare the fitness measurements to accepted health standards to ascertain the client's current fitness level. The results should allow the personal trainer to determine the order of training based on the area of greatest need. Explain the results to the client in a straightforward manner, to provide motivation for achieving goals. If any absolute or relative contraindications are present before exercise testing, stop immediately and refer the client to a physician. The same is true if a contraindication presents during exercise testing.

Referral to Physician

If exercise testing indicates that the client should seek a physician before continuing, the personal trainer should encourage it. If the client has an uncontrolled issue and is not currently seeing a physician, the personal trainer should be prepared to recommend some who are in the immediate area. Once medical care is established, the personal trainer should have an ongoing relationship with the physician to maintain the best care of the client. It is important for the physician to know what is happening in the exercise program, as it may change or affect the care she is providing.

Importance of Heart Rate and Ratings of Perceived Exertion (RPE)

Heart rate and ratings of perceived exertion (RPE) help the personal trainer monitor how hard the client is working. RPE correlates highly with the client's response to exercise. One way to make sure the client does not exceed the heart rate maximum recommended by his or her physician is by using the perceived exertion scale, a subjective test that allows the client to gauge his or her exertion level based on physical cues. The original scale ranged from 6 to 20. A 6 signified light exertion and a 20 indicated strenuous exertion. The old version was modified, and the new one runs from 0 (no exertion at all) through 11 (absolute top-level exertion).

Old version		New version	
6		0.0	No intensity
7	Very, very light	0.3	
8		0.5	Just noticeable
9	Very light	0.7	
10		1.0	
11	Fairly light	1.5	
12		2.0	Light
13	Somewhat hard	2.5	
14		3.0	
15	Hard	4.0	
16		5.0	Heavy
17	Very hard	6.0	
18		7.0	
19	Very, very hard	8.0	
20		9.0	
		10.0	Strongest intensity
		11.0	
			Highest possible

It is appropriate for the personal trainer to check client heart rate and assess RPE multiple times throughout the exercise session. The personal trainer must record heart rate and RPE; this will provide another way to keep track of how the client is progressing. Understanding these variables helps the personal trainer determine if an exercise is appropriate for the client's fitness level. If the exercise is too challenging, the trainer can modify the exercise so that it is suitable for the client, or if it is not challenging enough, the trainer can make the exercise more difficult to provide sufficient challenge for the client.

Normal and Abnormal Acute Responses to Cardiovascular Exercise

A normal response to cardiovascular exercise is for heart rate and systolic blood pressure to increase but for diastolic blood pressure to remain mostly unchanged. An abnormal response to cardiovascular exercise is indicated by the following:

- onset of angina or angina-like symptoms
- drop in systolic blood pressure of >10 mmHg from baseline measurements
- dramatic rise in blood pressure (systolic >250 mmHg, diastolic >115 mmHg)
- shortness of breath/wheezing and/or leg cramps
- indications of poor gas exchange (light-headedness, confusion, pallor, nausea, etc.)
- heart rate fails to increase with exercise intensity increase
- obvious change in the rhythm of the heart
- client asks to stop the exercise
- onset of severe fatigue
- the equipment fails to respond

Circumference Measurements

The standard circumference sites for measurement are as follows:

- abdomen
- arm
- buttocks/hips
- calf
- forearm
- hips/thigh
- mid-thigh
- And waist

Take measurements with a plastic, flexible measuring tape; the tape should not press hard enough on the skin to make an indentation. Go through each measurement site once, and then repeat a second time. The circumference waist measurement can be used to assess risk for disease. For females, <70 cm is associated with very low risk, 70–89 cm with low risk, 90–109 cm with high risk, and >110 cm with very high risk. For men, <80 cm is considered very low risk, 80–99 cm low risk, 100–120 cm high risk, and >120 cm very high risk. Higher circumference values indicate more fat storage and thus greater risk for disease.

Risk by Waist Circumference

Females		Males	
Waist Circumference	**Risk**	**Waist Circumference**	**Risk**
<70 cm	Very low risk	<80 cm	Very low risk
70–89 cm	Low risk	80–99 cm	Low risk
90–109 cm	High risk	100–120 cm	High risk
>110 cm	Very high risk	>120 cm	Very high risk

Skinfold Measurements

When selecting skinfold sites, the personal trainer must decide how many sites will be measured; there are options for 3 and 7 site measurements. All measurements should be made on the right side of the body with the client standing. The personal trainer should pinch the skin in each site, placing the calipers around the pinched skin halfway between the base and crest of the fold. The calipers should stay in place while reading the measurement, but no longer than 1–2 seconds. Duplicate measurements should be taken to ensure accuracy; it is best to rotate through the measurements so the skin can regain normal thickness and texture.

Circumference Measurements vs. Skinfold Measurements

Circumference and skinfold measurements follow a similar pattern in measurement sites; however, the circumference measurements use a tape measure rather than skin calipers. Circumference measurements are ideal for the extremely overweight client because they are easier to obtain than skinfold measurements. Circumference and skinfold measurements assess body fat with similar accuracy and are easy for personal trainers to complete in the field.

Assessing Safety in Muscular Strength, Endurance, and Power Tests

There are several variables for the personal trainer to consider when selecting the fitness tests for client assessment. The commonly accepted test criteria are objectivity, validity, reliability, economy, and safety. Safety includes age, medical history, injury history, diseases (and comorbidities), and any of the contraindications previously listed. If the client has joint problems such as arthritis or impaired mobility due to disease or spinal misalignment, the personal trainer must pick a proper version of each muscular test and decide when modifications are appropriate. A test should never be performed when a client is injured; wait for the client to make a full recovery to achieve the best test results. When training for resistance, a normative acute response for the client includes an increase in blood pressure and heart rate to divert blood to the working muscles.

Dangers of Training for Flexibility Outside a Joint's Proper Range of Motion

When training a client to meet flexibility goals, it is dangerous to exceed a joint's range of motion because ligaments and tendons may become damaged. In addition, if a client has led a sedentary life and is not in the habit of stretching, the muscles will be tight and stretching will need to progress in a gradual fashion. Consistency is crucial for increasing flexibility; incorporating a regular stretching reinforces the importance of stretching for the client and helps the client meet flexibility goals.

Assessment of Kyphosis, Lordosis, and Scoliosis

The personal trainer can elect to complete a postural analysis with the client. For kyphosis, the personal trainer can observe whether there is curvature of the thoracic spine and/or the neck slightly pushed forward. Lordosis can be observed by noting whether the client has an anterior or posterior tilt to the pelvis. Scoliosis can be observed by having the client stand against a wall that has horizontal lines on it. Observe whether the client tilts to the right or the left; one shoulder will appear farther away from the horizontal line than the other. If lines are not present on the fitness center wall, lines can be drawn on a poster board to hang on the wall. Knowing whether any of these issues are present will help the personal trainer troubleshoot potential range-of-motion issues.

Informing a Client of Exercise Testing Results

When discussing fitness testing results, discuss client strengths first to create a positive environment. For instance, if a client did well on the abdominal curl-up test, but poorly on the 1 RM bench press test, he is doing well in muscular endurance, but needs work in muscular strength. The trainer should praise the client for their muscular endurance, but stress the need to increase muscular strength. Focusing on strengths before addressing areas of weakness builds a positive foundation so the client can focus on making changes in areas where test results were negative. Conversely, a negative way to inform a client of exercise testing results is to discuss weak areas first. Discussing weaknesses first is demoralizing to the client if motivation to reach fitness goals is lacking. While it is important for the client to understand the truth about their fitness and health, it is important to convey the information in a manner that reinforces the notion that lasting change is a possibility.

Positively explaining fitness results to the client and setting goals designed to strengthen areas of weakness gives the personal trainer a way to assess the client's progress continually. Reassessing goals allows the client to clearly see the benefits of training, which leads to stronger motivation to stay faithful to the new habit. Positive progress also helps the client see the benefit of exercising independently and provides the ability to set additional goals and build healthy habits in other areas that need change. Seeing change in one area creates a positive feeling of control over life habits that was previously absent.

Developing a Reassessment Plan

Creating Achievable Goals

To create effective goals, the personal trainer must do the following:

- listen to what the client is saying
- assess the initial paperwork
- assess initial exercise capacity

Listening to the client allows the trainer to identify what the client wants to change. This is useful because the client will have a sense of ownership over the goal setting process. Initial paperwork will show if there are pre-existing conditions that to address with specific types of exercise. The initial exercise testing will further reveal weak areas of fitness that require attention.

Using Client Goals to Create a Workout Regimen and Troubleshoot Negative Behaviors

A client shares a goal of losing 20 lbs; in addition, the personal trainer realizes the client may have an uncontrolled metabolic disease. The client struggles with completing the 6-minute walk test and the 1 RM test, has an abdominal circumference measurement of 115 cm, but does well on her sit-and-reach and push-up tests. The trainer can set a primary goal that aims to increase the client's overall cardiovascular fitness and muscular strength. Once the goal has been set, the trainer can share with the client how reaching these goals will lead to the desired weight loss. Additionally, the personal trainer advises the client to seek medical attention because the paperwork indicates the possibility of an uncontrolled metabolic disease. If the client seems reluctant to show up on time to sessions, or go along with the personal trainer's suggestions, there are several options available for the personal trainer. The personal trainer can choose to verbally encourage the client's progress, have monetary penalties for missing training sessions without prior notice, create a reward system for goal maintenance, etc. The trainer should be creative with these options and choose one that fits the personality of the client.

Reassessment

Reassess goals at regular intervals to measure progress. There are a variety of methods to reassess goals. For instance, a personal trainer might take notes during each individual training session, but then reassess each goal with a fitness test every 6–12 weeks depending on the difficulty of the goal and how many sessions the client has completed. The personal trainer gains valuable information to convey to the client. When the client understands progress, they are motivated to continue working diligently in the sessions.

Exercise Programming and Implementation

Reviewing Client Information and Test Results

ACSM Risks and Benefits

It is important to understand the risks and benefits of exercise for adults, seniors, children/adolescents, and pregnant women because it allows the personal trainer to prescribe the correct fitness tests and design an effective exercise program. These guidelines serve as a road map for the trainer and client to see what the acceptable norms are for exercise. Knowledge of the risks and benefits helps the trainer know what will be most appropriate for the client for each session.

Exercise guidelines for otherwise healthy adults include the following: in general, adults should participate in fitness-related physical activity 3–5 days per week, enjoy leisure-related physical activity 2–3 days per week, and sit sparingly. The following exercise guidelines refer to seniors: in general, they should perform 30 minutes of moderate physical activity on most (or all) days of the week and should consult a physician before starting a more vigorous program. Flexibility and resistance training should be included on several days each week. For children, the following guidelines are applicable: have at least 60 minutes (up to two hours) of age appropriate physical activity on most (or all) days of the week. Activity should be moderate to vigorous and should be broken into 15-minute increments. Activities lasting longer than 2 hours are discouraged. For women who are pregnant, the following guidelines apply: moderate physical activity on most (orall) days of the week if there are no contraindications to exercise. In addition, regular exercise is encouraged; if a woman was previously sedentary, light intensity exercise is encouraged. Exercise in the supine position is discouraged after the first trimester.

ACSM Exercise Guidelines

Adults	Seniors	Children	Pregnant Women
Fitness-related physical activity 3-5 days per week	30 minutes of moderate physical activity most days of the week	At least 60 minutes of age-appropriate physical activity most days of the week	Moderate physical activity on most days of the week if there are no contraindications to exercise
Leisure-related physical activity 2-3 days per week	Should consult a physician before starting a more vigorous program	Moderate to vigorous activity broken into 15-minute increments	Regular exercise is encouraged
Sit sparingly	Flexibility and resistance training should be included several days each week	Activities should not exceed 2 hours in duration	If a woman was previously sedentary, light intensity exercise is encouraged
			Exercise in the supine position is discouraged after the first trimester

Clients Medically Cleared to Exercise with Chronic Disease

Many clients have a chronic disease but have been advised by their doctor to exercise. In such cases, specific guidelines apply to their exercise prescription. Clients who have arthritis are encouraged to perform cardiorespiratory training 3–5 days/week (20–60 min, large muscle groups), resistance 2-3 days/week (1 set of 3–20 repetitions, 8–10 exercises), and flexibility 5–7 days/week ideally (15-30 sec per stretch, all the major muscle groups, 2–4x each). Clients with diabetes mellitus are encouraged to perform cardiorespiratory training 3–4 days/week (20–60 min), resistance (2 days per week minimum with 48 hours of rest in between, 1 set of 15–20 repetitions for each major muscle group), and flexibility (every day ideally). Cleints with dyslipidemia are encouraged to perform cardiorespiratory training 5 or more days/week (40–60 min, primarily large muscle group aerobic activities), resistance 2–3 days/week (1 set of 3–20 repetitions, 8–10 exercises), and flexibility 5–7 days/week ideally (15–30 sec per stretch, all the major muscle groups, 2–4x each). Hypertensive clients follow a similar protocol as those with dyslipidemia with the following alterations: cardiorespiratory activity on 3–7 days/week (30–60 min), and resistance training should be combined with aerobic activity using lower resistance and higher repetitions. For obese patients, cardiorespiratory training should begin with moderate intensity, 45–60 min/session on 5-7 days/week. Obese patients may use resistance guidelines that apply to otherwise healthy adults.

- Arthritis
  - perform cardiorespiratory training 3–5 days/week (20–60 min, large muscle groups)
  - resistance 2–3 days/week (1 set of 3–20 repetitions, 8–10 exercises)
  - flexibility 5–7 days/week ideally (15–30 sec per stretch, all the major muscle groups, 2-4x each)

- Diabetes mellitus
    - perform cardiorespiratory training 3–4 days/week (20–60 min)
    - resistance (2 days per week minimum with 48 hours of rest in between, 1 set of 15–20 repetitions for each major muscle group)
    - flexibility (every day ideally)
- Patients with dyslipidemia
    - perform cardiorespiratory training 5 or more days/week (40–60 min, primarily large muscle group aerobic activities)
    - resistance 2–3 days/week (1 set of 3–20 repetitions, 8–10 exercises)
    - flexibility 5–7 days/week ideally (15–30 sec per stretch, all the major muscle groups, 2–4x each)
- Hypertensive clients
    - follow a similar protocol as those with dyslipidemia with the following alterations:
        - cardiorespiratory activity 3–7 days/week (30–60 min)
        - resistance training should be combined with aerobic activity using lower resistance and higher repetitions
- Obese clients
- cardiorespiratory training should begin with moderate intensity, 45–60 min/session on 5–7 days/week
- Obese patients may use resistance guidelines that apply to otherwise healthy adults

Individuals with metabolic syndrome may use the same guidelines as otherwise healthy adults unless there is a negative immune response to exercise; otherwise, adequate rest may be needed before continuing. Individuals with osteoporosis should incorporate the following: resistance activities 2 days/week with the load directed over the long axis of the bone (1–2 sets of 8–10 repetitions), flexibility training on most to all days of the week, and cardiorespiratory activity that is not high impact. Individuals with peripheral artery disease should have an extended warm-up (5–10 min) and walking should be the main form of cardiorespiratory activity (3–5 days/week). Resistance training should be complementary to other activity, not instead of the activity. Patients with pulmonary disease should have a minimum of 3–5 days/week of cardiorespiratory activity, and resistance guidelines are the same as otherwise healthy adults.

- Metabolic syndrome
    - use the same guidelines as otherwise healthy adults unless there is a negative immune response to exercise; otherwise, adequate rest may be needed before continuing.
- Osteoporosis
    - resistance activities 2 days/week with the load directed over the long axis of the bone (1–2 sets of 8–10 repetitions).
    - flexibility training on most to all days of the week, and cardiorespiratory activity that is not high impact.
- Peripheral artery disease
    - extended warm-up (5–10 min).
    - walking should be the main form of cardiorespiratory activity (3–5 days/week).
    - Resistance training should be complementary to other activity, not instead of the activity.
- Pulmonary disease.

- A minimum of 3–5 days/week of cardiorespiratory activity.
- Resistance guidelines are the same as otherwise healthy adults.

Physiological Responses During Exercise That May Require a Physician

The personal trainer should refer a client to a physician if the client experiences any of the following responses during exercise:

- angina or angina-like symptoms
- excessive drop in systolic blood pressure when workload remains constant
- shortness of breath and/or excessive cramping in the legs
- lightheadedness
- confusion
- nausea
- cyanosis
- heart rate does not increase even though exercise intensity increases
- an obvious change in heart rhythm

Any of these symptoms could indicate something more serious, and should be referred to a physician for follow-up.

Modifications During Initial Fitness Assessment

Certain clients may require modifications to complete the initial fitness assessment. Always consider the client's physical limitations and prioritize safety when administering fitness assessments. There are a variety of ways to modify an assessment. Common modifications include reducing the weight, performing an alternate exercise that is less challenging, and spotting. If a client has a disease that affects range of motion or ease of movement, it may be more beneficial to modify assessments or skip some assessments because the risk of injury outweighs the benefit to the client. In addition, obese clients may struggle to complete assessments for muscular endurance and strength or flexibility due to their weight. In such cases, it is acceptable to begin with the recommendations allowed for their population group. Although this list is incomplete, it illustrates the importance of modifying the exercise to accommodate the client's limitations and ensure safety.

Functional Fitness and Sports-Specific Training

Functional fitness refers to fitness exercises that mimic real life experiences and help prevent injury in those situations. For instance, for a client who experiences low back pain whenever she does things that require twisting of the spine, it is helpful for the personal trainer to incorporate movements that require twisting of the spine through different planes of movement and with varying resistance modalities to strengthen that area and train it in a new movement pattern. Sports-specific training emphasizes speed, strength, power, and endurance in athletic situations and also includes training specific to the sport in which the client participates. The average client does not necessarily need to engage in sports-specific training.

Balance Training

Balance training becomes more important as clients age, and is especially important if clients have diseases such as arthritis. Balance can be included as a separate section of the workout, or if the client is more advanced, it can be combined with other exercises. An example of balance training can be to simply balance on one leg for a certain amount of time. An example of a combined balance and resistance move could be to do a one-legged bicep curl. In addition, balance can be included in cardiovascular training by having clients walk up and down stairs without the use of the railing or walking backwards on an indoor track. Modifications for balance exercises can include providing support for the client by allowing him to hold on to the personal trainer's arm, wall, or railing.

Sports-Specific Training in Power and Strength

Sport-specific training for power emphasizes explosive movements. This can be achieved through jump training (plyometrics) and resistance training. Such examples would include jumping hurdles or doing jump squats, and using lighter weights but lifting as quickly or "explosively" as possible. Understanding the anaerobic system, including how long the client can exert maximal effort and the amount of time that is needed for recovery, allows the personal trainer to develop power more effectively. Developing strength requires recruiting more muscle fibers and improving neurological connections. This is accomplished by lifting heavy weights (85-100% of 1RM), which necessitates fewer repetitions. There are other variables to consider such as exercise selection, rest periods, and diet. For sports-specific strength the entire body is worked, but the muscles needing to be strengthened for sports performance are given special attention.

Anaerobic vs. Aerobic Training

The first stages of exercise initiate the anaerobic energy system. It converts food nutrients (primarily carbohydrates) into a fuel source, but it does not use oxygen to do so. Anaerobic exercise refers to short bouts of activity and includes resistance and plyometric training. Aerobic training uses oxygen to convert food nutrients (primarily carbohydrates) into usable energy. The aerobic system provides energy whenever exercise duration exceeds 2 minutes. Aerobic exercise tends to refer to endurance activities such as running or bicycling.

Precautions to Take During Extreme Weather Conditions

Extreme weather conditions requires special care if exercise testing or training takes place outside. When conditions are hot and humid, it is important that the clients hydrate sufficiently before starting exercise and are given plenty of opportunities to rehydrate during exercise. They should wear clothing that is moisture-wicking and avoid wearing cotton if at all possible. Clients should be given adequate rest periods. Clients should be observed for signs of heat stroke or heat exhaustion. ACSM identifies the characteristics of heat stroke as hot and dry skin, (but can be sweating); dyspnea; confusion; often unconscious. A heat stroke can result in death. According to ACSM, heat exhaustion is characterized by profuse sweating; cold and clammy skin; multiple muscle spasms; headache; nausea; loss of consciousness; dizziness; tachycardia; insecure gait; low blood pressure; body temperature normal to slightly increased. When conditions are cold and humid, the same instructions apply but with a few modifications. Clients should layer clothing that is moisture-wicking so they can remove it as their body warms up. Additionally, the warm-up should be lengthened to prepare the muscles adequately. In either situation, personal trainers should monitor the clients closely, as they will not always be assertive when they need hydration or if they feel light-headed or dizzy.

Common Heat Illness Symptoms

Heat Stroke	Heat exhaustion
Hot and dry skin (but can be sweating)	Profuse sweating
Dyspnea	Cold and clammy skin
Confusion	Multiple muscle spasms
Unconscious	Headache
	Nausea
	Loss of consciousness
	Dizziness
	Tachycardia
	Insecure gait
	Low blood pressure
	Body temperature normal to slightly increased

Training at Moderate and High Altitudes

At higher altitudes, it is important to ensure that clients remain hydrated. When a client feels cold, they may not necessarily feel thirsty. Higher altitudes can quickly cause dehydration if the client waits until they feel thirsty to drink. Feelings of fatigue can also be increased as less oxygen is binding to the hemoglobin molecules in the client's blood. Frequent breaks may be in order, and if the client is traveling to moderate or high altitude and intends to exercise, they must be aware that they may not be able to exercise at the same capacity. The client also needs to schedule water breaks even when if they are not thirsty. It is important to drink water throughout the day to stay adequately hydrated for the next exercise session.

Recording Client Progress

Recording client progress at the end of each exercise session provides the personal trainer with a small picture of how the client is performing from session to session. At the time of reassessment and re-testing, the trainer can then compare results with session notes. This gives the trainer and the client a full picture of progress. In addition, it is necessary for the personal trainer to provide ample documentation to a cooperating physician for liability reasons and so the physician is as informed as possible.

Selecting Modalities

Choosing Appropriate Exercises for Specific Goals

The personal trainer designs exercise sessions around one or more client goals. If the focus is a primary goal, it may be necessary to center the entire session on that goal, to ensure the goal is met. With secondary goals, it may be effective to group them together for a session. The client is more invested in each workout when they know what goals are being worked on and why. Awareness of the relationship between exercise selection and the achievement of goals increases motivation and faithfulness to the exercise routine.

Program Design and Session and Long-Term Goals

Program design must be appropriate for the client's current fitness level. It will not benefit the client or the trainer if session goals do not match long-term goals. Because session goals are building blocks that help the client reach the overall goals, they must align closely with overall goals. The program design must properly reflect both the session and overall goals. It is beneficial for the trainer to convey the specific goals for each session in written and verbal form.

Interval, Continuous, and Circuit Training Programs

Interval training for cardiovascular fitness involves changing speed or grade at various time intervals. Continuous training involves staying at a similar speed or grade throughout the entire activity. Circuit training involves completing multiple exercises in sequential fashion (in a circuit) with minimal rest between sets, which keeps the heart rate elevated for an extended period. The resulting elevated heart rate provides the client cardiovascular benefit. Each of these training types can benefit cardiovascular fitness. For sedentary individuals, continuous training is helpful when it is maintained at low to moderate intensities because it will build endurance, encourage weight loss, and condition heart rate. Interval training provides challenges and increases caloric expenditure while challenging the client's cardiovascular system. Circuit training combines resistance activities with cardiovascular activities and helps build strength as well as endurance. As with any training modality, clients will reach a plateau in their performance if the same training routine is continued for too long. A well-rounded fitness program that emphasizes all components of fitness is always desirable. Neglecting any fitness component adversely affects the body. If one area of fitness is emphasized over another, the neglected area will suffer consequently (e.g. cardiorespiratory fitness suffers if muscular fitness is stressed, and vice versa).

Interval and circuit training build stamina and endurance. Client limitations should always be considered when designing a program, and appropriate modalities should always be selected regardless of client goals.

Energy Systems Used

The aerobic system is the primary responder during extended activity. It is the primary energy system used in continuous training (i.e. staying at a similar speed or grade throughout the entire activity). During interval and circuit training, the anaerobic or the aerobic system can provide the primary source of energy depending on the duration of the activity. Circuit stations lasting for less than 2 minutes with at least 30 seconds to 1 minute of rest between stations use anaerobic pathways to supply the energy through the ATP-PC and glycolytic pathways. If station rotations are longer than 2 minutes in duration (or there is less rest between circuits), the aerobic system is the primary energy pathway.

Rest Within Circuit Training

In circuit training, rest performs a very important function because it determines which energy pathway system is used. The rest periods between stations allow the anaerobic system to "reload" to fuel the next set of exercises. In this way, rest is related to intensity. Maximum exertion reuires replenished enrgy sources, which is contingent on adequate rest. Without adequate rest, the client will be unable to provide sufficient exertion to deplete energy stores and tax the anaerobic system. It is important for the personal trainer to understand that rest plays a large part in the training of the anaerobic system.

Relation of Activities of Daily Living (ADLs) to Long-Term Fitness Goals

When the personal trainer is assessing and creating long-term client goals, it is important to assess how the client feels about normal life activities. The personal trainer can ask questions about leisure time activities, whether they feel physically capable of doing the things they enjoy, or whether any common activities (i.e., sitting or standing for long periods of time) cause unnecessary discomfort. The personal trainer must incorporate exercises that address these issues as they directly correlate to the client's quality of life. Improving the client's quality of life allows them to see that exercise enables them to do the things they enjoy. Ideally, strengthens habits and serves as a source of motivation. Activities of daily living can shape short- and long-term goals.

Activity and Training Recommendations for Different Goals

For general cardiovascular and strength benefits, clients can follow the guidelines as set forth by ACSM for cardiovascular and muscular fitness and flexibility. It is recommended that clients expend at least 2000 kcal per week in physical activity to lose weight. To gain weight, clients need to focus on resistance training for hypertrophy. In addition, diet plays a role for goals involving losing and gaining weight. To promote weight loss, caloric ingestion must be regulated and decreased, and activity levels must increase. Caloric ingestion must be increased to gain weight, but it must come from nutritious foods. To improve fitness level and increase athletic performance, clients can focus on the specific variables, such as hypertrophy, power, endurance, and speed training that best fit their personal goals. The key to obtaining results with clients is creating workouts that are challenging and not too comfortable for them.

Exercise Recommendations for Healthy Adults

Frequency	Types of Exercises
2–3 d/wk	Muscular strength and endurance, resistance exercise, calisthenics, balance, and agility exercise
At least 3 d/wk	Vigorous intensity aerobic activities (cardiovascular endurance), weight-bearing exercise, flexibility exercise
3–5 d/wk	A combination of moderate- and vigorous-intensity aerobic activities, weight-bearing exercise, flexibility exercise
At least 5 d/wk	Moderate intensity aerobic activities, weight-bearing exercise, flexibility exercise

Aerobic Exercises to Improve Physical Fitness

Recommended for adults who:	Exercise	Examples
All adults	Endurance activities requiring minimal skill or physical fitness to perform	Walking, leisurely cycling, aqua-aerobics, slow dancing
Have a regular exercise program and/or at least average physical fitness	Vigorous-intensity endurance activities requiring minimal skill	Jogging, running, rowing, aerobics, spinning, elliptical exercise, stepping exercise, fast dancing
Have acquired skill and/or at least average physical fitness levels	Endurance activities requiring skill to perform	Swimming, cross-country skiing, skating
Have a regular exercise program and at least average physical fitness	Recreational sports	Racquet sports, basketball, soccer, downhill skiing, hiking

Advanced Methods of Resistance Training

When a client has demonstrated that they are ready for advanced forms of resistance training, the personal trainer can introduce methods such as super sets, Olympic-style lifts, plyometrics, pyramid training, drop set training, contrast training, complex system, lactate tolerance system, or negative set system. Every client is unique, and the trainer must exercise judgement when progressing an exercise or program. Generally, the client should only progress to more complex resistance training methods after mastering the basic resistance movements. If the progression is too challenging, the client trainer should slow the progression until it is safe to proceed. Olympic-style movements train clients for quick, explosive movements that lift heavier weights. Plyometrics, also known as "jump training," trains for speed and power through different styles of explosive jumps. Pyramid sets begin with high volume and low weight. Subsequent sets lower volume and increase weight. Drop set training is a system that uses the same exercise performed to volitional failure in one set; then the weight is lowered, and the exercise is repeated. Contrast training combines strength and power training by completing one exercise until volitional failure; a similar movement is then performed with a lighter weight at a faster pace. Complex training combines agonist/antagonist exercises to fatigue a certain muscle to encourage hypertrophy. The lactate tolerance system has the goal of finishing a predetermined workout in the shortest amount of time possible. The negative set system encourages the exerciser to lift a heavier weight than normal, control the eccentric contraction, and have a spotter assist her with the concentric contraction.

Forms of Resistance Training

Olympic-style movements	train clients for quick, explosive movements that lift heavier weights
Plyometrics (jump training)	trains for speed and power through different styles of explosive jumps
Pyramid sets	begin with high volume and low weight, then increase to low volume with high weight through each subsequent set.
Drop set training	is a system that uses the same exercise performed to volitional failure in one set, then the weight is lowered and the exercise is repeated.

Contrast training	combines strength and power training by completing one exercise until volitional failure; a similar movement is then per-formed with a lighter weight but faster pace.
Complex training	combines agonist/antagonist exercises to fatigue a certain muscle to encourage hypertrophy.
Lactate tolerance system	has the goal of finishing a predetermined workout in the shortest amount of time possible.
Negative set system	encourages the exerciser to lift a heavier weight than normal, control the eccentric contraction, and have a spotter assist her with the concentric contraction.

Fitness Components Related to Motor Skill

Agility refers to a client's ability to explosively perform several different power movements one after another and in opposing directions; for example, zigzagging. Balance refers to a client's ability to control his body position while either standing still or moving. Reaction time means the client can react quickly to exercise stimulus or verbal instruction and change his movement pattern accordingly. Speed is quickness of movement, and power refers to explosive contractions of the muscles. Coordination can be thought of as the client's ability to perform the aforementioned components effectively, leading to efficient movement. More specifically, the ACSM defines coordination as the ability to use the senses, such as sight and hearing, together with body parts in performing tasks smoothly and accurately.

Physical Limitations and Contraindications

The trainer should prescribe exercises that are appropriate for the client. It is important to consider physical limitations and health issues that may contraindicate a client's ability to perform an exercise. If an exercise results in pain or siccomfort, it should be discontinued. If a client has bad knees or shoulders or back, is morbidly obese, and is unfamiliar with exercise in general, the following types of exercises should be avoided: squats, planks, reverse crunches, plyometrics. Clients need to be started with exercises that are simple before moving on to exercises that are more complex. In addition, clients may need the extra core support that standard resistance machines give before moving on to body-weight exercises that are unsupported. Beginning with these sorts of exercises increases the risk for injury.

Contraindications for Yoga, Proprioceptive Neuromuscular Facilitation (PNF), Static Stretching

One of the many benefits of yoga is improved flexibility. Most yoga positions can be modified if a client lacks the flexibility to perform a more complex movement Yoga might be contraindicated if the client has greatly reduced flexibility, has an injury, or has had joint or back surgery. In these instances, it is wise to advise the client to consult a physician and assess whether the potential benefit would outweigh the risk. PNF or static stretching might be contraindicated for the client if joints are inflamed; if stretching causes excessive pain; or if she currently has an infection, a vascular or acute injury, joint instability, or a disease that affects the tissue being stretched. If in doubt, consult medical personnel before beginning a stretching regimen.

Contraindications for High-Intensity, High-Impact Cardiovascular Exercises

Clients with a chronic disease that compromises their joints, an acute injury, acute infection, or a physical issue that may be exacerbated by beginning a high-intensity regimen should avoid High-intensity, high-impact cardiovascular exercises. For most clients, moderate physical activity is sufficient for health benefits and disease reduction. The personal trainer must assess the benefits/risk ratio for his client.

Determining Frequency, Intensity, Time, and Type of Exercise

Recommendations for Overall Fitness

Healthy Adults and Seniors

In general, the client should engage in cardiorespiratory activity 3–5 days/week, resistance training 2–3 days/week, and flexibility (ideally) 5–7days/week. Each activity should emphasize the major muscle groups. Ideally, cardiorespiratory training should occur at a range of 12–16 on the RPE scale, and resistance exercise should occur at a range of 19–20 RPE with the intent to reach volitional failure. Stretches should be held for 15–30 seconds each, with each muscle group being stretched 2–4 times at each session.

FITT Framework for Aerobic Exercise (aligned with the Physical Activity Guidelines for Americans)

Physical Activity Level	Classification	Frequency		Intensity			Time	
		Kcal/week	Days/week	HRR/$\dot{V}O_2R$	%MAX HR	RPE	Duration	Daily Steps
Sedentary	Poor	500-1000	3-5	30%-45%	57%-67%	Light-moderate	20-30 min/day	3000-3500
Minimal physical activity	Poor-Fair	1000-1500	3-5	40%-55%	64%-74%	Light-moderate	30-60 min/day	3000-4000
Sporadic physical activity	Fair-Average	1500-2000	3-5	55%-70%	74%-84%	Moderate-Hard	30-90 min/day	3000-4000
Habitual physical activity	Average-Good	2000	3-5	65%-80%	80%-91%	Moderate-Hard	30-90 min/day	3000-4000
High amounts of habitual activity	Good-Excellent	2000	3-5	70%-85%	84%-94%	Somewhat Hard-Hard	30-90 min/day	3000-4000

Exercise Recommendations for Healthy Seniors

Cardio

HR	Exertion	Duration	Type
Moderate (e.g., 40%-60% heart rate reserve [HRR]) to vigorous (e.g., 60%-90% HRR) intensity aerobic exercise is recommended for most adults, and light (e.g., 30%-40% HRR) to moderate intensity aerobic exercise can be beneficial in individuals who are deconditioned	Assess appropriateness of heart rate ranges using a scale of 0-10 for level of physical exertion, 3-4 for light intensity, 5-6 for moderate intensity and 7-8 for vigorous intensity.	For moderate intensity, physical activities, accumulate at least 30 or up to 60 (for greater benefit) min/day in bouts of at least 10 minutes each to total 150-300 min/week, or at least 20-30 min/day of more vigorous intensity, physical activities to total 75-100 min/week or an equivalent combination of moderate and vigorous intensity, physical activity. Lower ranges are for adults who have not participated in any exercise program, or for frail individuals.	Any modality that does not impose excessive orthopedic stress - walking is the most common type of activity. Aquatic exercise and stationary cycle exercise may be advantageous for those with limited tolerance for weight-bearing activity.

Strength

Frequency	Intensity	Type
2 days/week	Moderate intensity (i.e., 60%-70% one repetition maximum [1-RM]). Light intensity (i.e., 40%-50% 1-RM) for older adults beginning a resistance training program. When 1-RM is not measured, intensity can be prescribed between moderate (5-6) and vigorous (7-8) intensity on a scale of 0-10.	Progressive weight-training program or weight-bearing calisthenics (8-10 exercises involving the major muscle groups; 1 set of 10-15 repetitions each), stair climbing, and other strengthening activities that use the major muscle groups.

Flexibility

Frequency	Intensity	Time	Type
2 days/week	Stretch to the point of feeling tightness or slight discomfort.	Hold stretch for 30-60 seconds	Any physical activities that maintain or increase flexibility using slow movements that terminate in sustained stretches for each major muscle group using static stretches rather than rapid ballistic movements

Healthy Children and Adolescents

Children should accumulate 60 minutes to several hours of moderate and vigorous physical activity on most days of the week. There should be several periods of activity during the day that last 15 minutes or more and all activities should be age appropriate. Extended periods of activity that last longer than 2 hours are not encouraged during the day due to heat considerations.

ACSM Guidelines for Healthy Children and Adolescents

Frequency	At least 3–4 days per week (preferably daily)
Intensity	Moderate (physical activity that noticeably increases breathing, sweating, and HR) to vigorous (physical activity that substantially increases breathing, sweating, and HR) intensity.
Time	30 min of moderate and 30 min of vigorous intensity to total 60 min of accumulated physical activity.
Type	A variety of activities that are enjoyable and developmentally appropriate for the child or adolescent; these may include walking, active play/games, dance, sports, and muscle- and bone-strengthening activities.

Healthy Pregnant Women

Pregnant women who are healthy are encouraged to engage in 30–40 minutes of physical activity on most to all days of the week. Women who were sedentary before becoming pregnant can begin an exercise regimen that is light. Exercise in the supine position after the first trimester should be avoided due to slightly obstructed venous return that lowers cardiac output and could cause orthostatic hypotension.

ACSM Guidelines for Healthy Pregnant Women

Frequency	At least three—and preferably all—days of the week.
Intensity	Moderate intensity (40%–60% VO_2 Reserve). Because of heart rate (HR) variability during pregnancy, consider using the rating of perceived exertion (RPE) (12–14 on a scale of 6–20) or the "talk test" (being able to maintain a conversation during activity) to monitor exercise intensity. HR ranges that correspond to moderate-intensity exercise have also been developed for pregnant women based on age.
Time	At least 15 min gradually increasing to at least 30 min of accumulated moderate intensity physical activity to total 150 minutes per week.
Type	Dynamic, rhythmic physical activities that use the large muscle groups, such as walking and cycling.

Adults with Cardiovascular Disease but Medically Cleared to Exercise

If clients have a chronic heart disease that is stable, they generally need an extended warm-up (5–10 minutes), resistance exercises 2 days/week that include all the major muscle groups (clients should perform 1 set of 10–15 repetitions to moderate fatigue and use 8–10 different exercises; weight should be increased at a rate of 2–5 lbs per week for arms and 5–10 lbs per week for legs), and cardiovascular activity 3–4 times weekly (in addition to an increase in daily total energy expenditure) that is moderate intensity. For the greatest benefits, 5–6 hours of cardiovascular activity per week is recommended. Stretching all the major muscle groups on a daily basis (15–30 sec each, 2–4 stretches per muscle group) is encouraged.

Adults with Metabolic Syndrome but Medically Cleared for Exercise

For clients who have a metabolic syndrome but are medically cleared for exercise, their goals should include the following: cardiorespiratory activity 3–4 days/week, lasting 20–60 minutes, at an intensity of 50–80% of their HRR. Resistance training should emphasize lower resistance and lower intensity: 1 set of 10–15 repetitions for each of the major muscle groups, increasing to 15–20 repetitions. Stretching of all the major muscle groups (15–30 sec each, 2–4 stretches per muscle group) should be emphasized on a daily basis.

Adults with Chronic Pain and Arthritis but Medically Cleared to Exercise

For adults who suffer from arthritis or other joint pain, their exercise prescription is as follows: cardiorespiratory (3–5 days/week, 20–60 min duration, large muscle groups emphasized), resistance (2–3 days/week, 1 set of 3–20 repetitions, 8–10 total exercises that cover all the major muscle groups), flexibility (preferred: 5–7 days/week, 15–30 sec each, 2–4 stretches for each major muscle group). Overstretching should be discouraged; morning exercise depends on a client-by-client basis, based on whether they find it helpful or not.

Importance of Accurate Medical History

It is important to have an accurate medical history for all clients. This information should be obtained during the initial client assessment. Complete and accurate medical history provides many benefits. Knowledge of medical history allows the client to design a program that is appropriate for the client. The personal trainer can prescribe exercises that avoid exacerbating medical issues, which benefits the client and insulates the trainer from liability issues. The trainer will also understand what medications the client is on and how they may affect exercise. Additionally, the personal trainer will be aware of potential triggers for worsening any existing medical conditions.

Exercise Modifications

When an exercise is too challenging or not challenging enough, the personal trainer should modify the exercise, so that is it appropriate for the client. It is the personal trainer's responsibility to observe the client and ask questions to make sure the intensity or the type of exercise is appropriate for the client; some clients have a "pain is gain" mentality and may not volunteer that the exercise is too difficult for them. It is important for the trainer to dispel this myth through education. Pain is a sign that that the body is injured and should not be ignored. Pain is not an effective indicator of workout intensity or effectiveness. Methods such as heart rate monitoring, ratings of perceived exertion, one rep maximum, and the talk test are the preferred measures of intensity that the trainer will use to ensure effective workouts. Fitness testing, body measurements, and increased capacity are better signs of a workout's efficacy. Likewise, clients new to exercise may not realize if an exercise is too easy for them, they may simply appreciate that they do not feel horrible as they exercise. The personal trainer must educate clients on the benefits of an appropriately challenging workout.

Components and Appropriate Flow of an Exercise Program

An exercise session should start with an adequate warm-up of the large muscle groups that will also increase the heart rate and prepare the body for what is to come. Depending upon the client, static stretches may be appropriate after the warm-up. Resistance activity should come next. Performing resistance training before cardiovasuclar activity limits fatigue which can compromise attention to proper technique and personal trainer cues. Cardiovascular activity should follow resistance training. The workout should conclude with a cool-down, and static stretches.

Exercises for Major Muscle Groups

The following exercises would be appropriate for the major muscle groups: chest (push-ups), upper back (double arm row), abdominal muscles (abdominal curl-ups), lower back (good morning), quadriceps group and hamstring group (weighted squats), calves (calf raises), shoulders (shoulder raises), biceps (biceps curls), and triceps (triceps dips).

Sample of Exercises for Major Muscle Groups

Chest	Shoulders	Upper Back	Lats	Biceps	Triceps	Quadriceps	Hamstrings	Gluteals	Abs
Barbell Bench Press	Military Press	Bent-Over Row	Pull-Up	Chin-Up	Triceps Dip	Barbell Squat	Romanian Deadlift	Barbell Lunge	Knee Raise
Incline Barbell Bench Press	Dumbbell Overhead Press	Shrug	Bent-Over Row	Incline Dumbbell Curl	Close Grip Bench Press	Front Squat	Lunge	Dumbbell Lunge	Crunch
Decline Barbell Bench Press	Stability Ball Press	Seated Row	Straight-Arm Pulldown	One-Arm Preacher Curl	Cable Press Down	Sumo Squat	Stability Ball Leg Curl	Single-Leg Squat	Stability Ball Crunch
Dumbbell Fly	Push Press	Upright Row	Lat Pull-Down	EZ-Bar Curl	Triceps Kickback	Lateral lunge	Jump Lunge	Floor Bridge	Reverse Crunch
Incline Dumbbell Fly	Arnold Press	Single-Arm Row	Dumbbell Pull-Over	Hammer Curl	Skullcrushers	Hack Squat	Lateral Lunge and Touch	Bulgarian Split Squat	Plank
Cable Crossover	Lateral Raise			Isolation Curl	Stability Ball Overhead	BOSU Squat			Side Plank
Cable Press	Stability Ball Lateral Raise			Standing Dumbbell Curl	TRX Extensions				Jack Knife
Dumbbell Bench Press	Front Raise			BOSU Curl					Figure Four Sit-up
Incline Dumbbell Bench Press	Stability Ball Front Raise			Cable Curl					
Stability Ball Dumbbell Press	Reverse Dumbbell Fly			21s					
Push-Up	Scaption			TRZ Curl					
Push-Up with Clap	Stability Ball Scaption								
Stability Ball Push-Up	Chicken Wings								
BOSU Push-Up	Reverse Cable Crossovers								
TRX Push-Up									
Hammer Machine									
Hammer Incline Machine									

Monitoring Response to Exercise

During exercise, there are various ways that a personal trainer can monitor a client's response to exercise. The RPE scale is an efficient way of assessing whether the workload is too challenging or not challenging enough for the client. Paying attention to physical signs of distress, such as labored breathing, pallor, dizziness, or sharp pain, can also be indicators that something more serious may be occurring. Heart rate is an effective and more accurate tool to measure the client's response to exercise. It is simple to administer and the cleint can be taught to measure their own heart rate.

Maximum Heart Rate and Heart Rate Reserve

To find the maximum heart rate, simply take the client's age and subtract it from the number 220. The resulting number is the age-adjusted maximum heart rate. To find the heart rate reserve (HRR), take the client's age and subtract it from 220. Take the resulting number, and subtract the resting pulse from it. This is the heart rate reserve. If training according to a percentage of the client's heart rate reserve, multiply the HRR by the percentage desired for training, then add the resting pulse to it. **Example:** A 60-year-old client needs to be trained at 70% of his HRR, his resting pulse is 65: 220 – 60 (age) = 160 (age-adjusted maximum heart rate); 160 – 65 (resting pulse) = 95; 95 x .70 = 66.5 + 65 (resting pulse) = 131.5 bpm. This client should have the goal of 131 bpm for training at 70% of his HRR.

Target Heart Rates for Different Medical Considerations

Several factors including fitness level, fitness goals, and chronic disease determine the specific training zone that the client trains in. Specific training zones are expressed as a percentage of HRR. Cardiac patients should have a goal of training up to 85% of HRR. For managing hypertension, training at 40% to 70% of HRR is recommended. For clients with arthritis, it is recommended to train at 50% to 85% of HRR. Diabetic clients should train at 50% to 80% of HRR. For clients with dyslipidemia, it is recommended to train at 40% to 70% of their HRR. For obese clients, initial exercise should have the goal of being at 40% to 60% of HRR; progression to higher intensities (50% to 75% of HRR) is recommended. For clients with osteoporosis, it is recommended to pursue non-impact activities at 40% to 70% of HRR.

Affliction	Target Heart Rate
Cardiac	85% of HRR
Hypertension	40% to 70% of HRR
Arthritis	50% to 85% of HRR
Diabetes	50% to 80% of HRR
Dyslipidemia	40% to 70% of their HRR
Obesity	40% to 60% of HRR (progressing to 75% of HRR)
Osteoporosis	non-impact activities at 40% to 70% of HRR

Periodized Training

Periodization of a training regimen is highly effective because it prevents the negative impact of general adaptation syndrome. Specifically, it assures that the same routine is not employed to the point that the body learns to cope, thus reducing ongoing training gains. Periodization can improve fitness gains while reducing injuries from repetitive actions. It also gives variations training type, volume, and frequency, opening the door for more interesting and thoughtful programs that keep the client motivated and involved. Even though periodization has been shown to work well, many health and fitness professionals do not use it in their training programs. This means that the training programs they use are repetitive, which can result in overuse injuries and a plateau effect in training. These results, in turn, can lead to low client motivation and cessation of regular training.

Periodized training allows the personal trainer to focus on goals such as endurance and hypertrophy with a client while avoiding overtraining. For example, a period of 12 weeks can be broken down into 3 periods of 4 weeks in each period. Through these different periods, the trainer varies the client's intensity, frequency, and duration of exercise so that a plateau is not reached, but maximal hypertrophy and endurance is attained. Injury risk is reduced because the client is rotating training styles and targeted muscle groups. Periodized training also helps those clients concerned with increasing different exercise variables such as speed, strength, and power.

In a periodized training schedule, the personal trainer can vary the goal within each period so that muscular power, hypertrophy, endurance, and strength can be achieved without reaching a plateau. For the goal of power, high-intensity, short-interval exercises should be included with the goal of most movements being explosive rather than static. Moderate-intensity sessions should be in between the power sessions to promote recovery. For hypertrophy, resistance training should be with a moderate-intensity weight, 10–15 repetitions, with rest of 30–60 seconds between sets. Endurance activities can be coupled with hypertrophy training and should be between 30–60 minutes for 4–6 days per week at moderate intensity, or 30–60 minutes 2–3 days per week for higher training intensities. Strength training should be done with higher resistance than hypertrophy training. The goal should be 2–3 sets of 6–8 repetitions, where the client feels tired with the last 2 repetitions. Additionally, exercises should be specific to the client's sport goals if they have any.

Repetition Maximum Test

The 1 RM test measures the greatest amount of resistance that the client can move through a full range of motion while still in control of the weight. This can provide a measure of either upper body or lower body strength. The benefit of knowing the client's 1 RM allows the personal trainer accurately estimate submaximal resistance loads with which to begin training and the 1RM serves as a measure of intensity (expressed as a percentage of 1RM). An example of the 1 RM test for the upper body is a bench press; an example of the 1 RM test for the lower body is the leg press.

Instructing the Client on Performing Exercises Safely

Resistance Exercises to Build Strength

Resistance exercises can help build muscular strength and endurance. When the appropriate exercises are performed, a client can complete daily living activities more easily, deter rapid bone loss, and reduce the risk for joint disease. Resistance training works along with cardiovascular training to decrease fat mass and increase lean mass. Increased resistance exercises break down the muscles by creating micro-tears in the tissue; the proper recovery period helps to rebuild those tissues and increase strength and hypertrophy. Increased muscle mass has the added benefit of increasing resting metabolic rate (i.e. muscle burns calories at rest), meaning an individual burns more calories when they build lean muscle. Estimates of the affect that lean muscle has on resting metabolic rate vary. Some conservative calculations show that a pound of muscle burns 6 calories per day, while more aggressive estimates indicate that an extra pound of lean muscle results in a 50 calorie per day jump in resting metabolic rate.

Effects of Cardiovascular Training on Activities of Daily Living and Endurance Activities

Cardiovascular training strengthens the heart and allows it to pump blood more effectively. Resting heart rate and blood pressure lower in response to cardiovascular training. During exercise, heart rate and blood pressure take longer to increase as the body handles the workload more efficiently. Clients will notice that commitment to an exercise routine makes it easier to perform daily activities, and daily activities can be performed without pain or fatigue serving as limiting factors. Clients will also notice better quality of sleep and feel more energetic. For endurance activities, clients will notice that they can exercise for longer periods of time, increase their speed, and adapt to training stimulus more quickly.

Effects of Exercise on Motor Skills and Coordination

As clients exercise, they will notice a positive effect on motor skills and coordination. With specific training in each of the following areas: resistance, flexibility, cardiovascular, and balance, clients will have increased quality of life. Coordination and motor skills are improved when speed and balance activities are included in the training regimen. Balance training can be incorporated in resistance training (e.g., completing a bicep curl while standing on one leg) or in cardiovascular activities (e.g., power skips or bicycling) and trains clients to use their fine and gross motor skills to complete the movement. As more movements are practiced in an exercise session, the client becomes more efficient clients at performing them, and their motor skills and coordination will continue to improve.

Demonstration of Expected Movement Patterns

To ensure the client understands exactly what to do for an exercise, the personal trainer needs to physically demonstrate the movement pattern as well as provide verbal and nonverbal cues. It is never appropriate for the trainer to assume the client understands based on verbal instruction alone. An example of a verbal cue is to give instructions explaining how to complete an exercise. An example of a nonverbal cue would be personally demonstrating the exercise or helping the client complete the movement.

Demonstration of Proper Range of Motion

There are several important concepts related to range of motion that the trainer must understanf. Flexibility refers to the level to which a person can extend the muscles and soft tissues, allowing the joint a full range of motion. Dynamic functional flexibility refers to the cycle of flexibility that comes from extensibility, which allows for a wide range of motion of a joint, coupled with optimal communication between the nervous system and the muscles. Extensibility refers to the general ability of muscles and soft body tissues to stretch or be elastic. Dynamic range of motion refers to the body's ability to move freely in all planes of movement coupled with the ability of the nervous system to handle and control these movements in a safe manner. It is important for the client to train in a manner that promotes an efficient range of motion to maximize performance and minimize injury risk. Demonstrating proper range of motion helps the client to remain free from injury. One resistance exercise that is often done incorrectly is the lat pull. People will typically pull the bar down behind their neck and head. Although the glenohumeral joint can rotate 360 degrees, it is not advisable to train by bringing the arms behind the head in this manner. Proper form requires lowering the bar in front of the face and neck but not leaning back away from the bar. Performing this exercise improperly often leads to overuse injuries in the shoulder joint that could become serious enough for medical attention.

Benefits of Using Several Different Resistance Modalities

Specificity is the principle that states all training adaptations are specific to the stimulus applied. The take away from this principle is that the body will adapt to meet the demands that are placed on it. The trainer must design a program that challenges the client's body to adapt in the desired fashion. This also gives the client a taste of the variety resistance training can offer. Additionally, muscles can be trained in different ways depending on the goal of strength, hypertrophy, endurance, or power, and it becomes less likely that a plateau will occur for the client. Examples of different resistance modalities include the following:

- Constant resistant devices
  - The resistance remains the same through the range of motion.
  - Example: Free Weights
- Variable resistance devices
  - The resistance is altered through the range of motion.
  - Example: Cams and Levers
- Accommodating resistance devices
  - Allows maximum exertion through the entire range of motion.
  - Example: Specially designed machinery
- Static resistance devices
  - The weight does not move (isotonic).
  - Example: Pushing against and immovable object.

It is necessary for the personal trainer to monitor the client constantly during the performance of each movement. Spotting is appropriate and requires verbal and nonverbal cues to ensure the client is performing each movement as safely as possible.

Nontraditional Training Activity

For some clients, nontraditional training may be in order; this can include:

- Stability balls are large inflatable balls that are used to improve core strength and balance.
- Balance boards encompass any unstable platform that challenges balance and improves proprioception and coordination.
- Resistance bands are large (usually rubber) bands, staps, or cables that are used to build muscular strength.

- Medicine balls are heavy balls used to build strength and power.
- Foam rollers are cylindrical tubes of varying density that are used for self myofascial release (SMR).

These pieces of equipment are useful for clients who are rehabilitating from injury, are elderly, are incapacitated in any way, or need to work on their balance. Additionally, it provides a way to change a movement and make it more complex so as to increase the intensity of the workout for clients. Using this type of equipment is also considered functional training and helps clients achieve ease of movement and greater strength in activities of daily living.

Dangers of the Valsalva Maneuver

The Valsalva maneuver occurs when a client holds his breath during a resistance or cardiovascular exercise. This is dangerous because it causes a sharp increase in blood pressure and heart rate, which can lead to the client becoming light-headed or dizzy and passing out. Clients need to learn to breathe appropriately during cardiovascular exercises and during the eccentric and concentric phases of resistance training to avoid the Valsalva maneuver.

Biomechanics of Resistance Training, Yoga, and Running

A trainer should strive to prescribe resistance training and yoga that challenges the spine to move through all planes of movement (i.e. frontal, sagittal, and transverse planes) in a variety of ways including bending, twisting, and stretching. Yoga uses almost exclusively isometric training (but can incorporate isotonic exercises), while resistance training utilizes primarily isometric training (but can include isotonic actions). Isokinetic training involves sophisticated equipment and is not common in a gym setting. Both resistance training and yoga can exert compressive forces on the spine, and care must be taken to protect vulnerable areas. During running, the spine should stay relatively stable with little to no twisting and no bending or stretching, and should only move through the frontal plane.

During human locomotion, the heel strikes the ground first, and the rest of foot flattens out. Next, the heel lifts off the ground. In the final stage, the heel rises until the toe lifts off the ground. Proper frontside mechanics include includes ankle dorsiflexion, knee flexion, hip flexion, and a neutral pelvis. The backside mechanics involve proper alignment of the rear leg and pelvis which includes ankle plantarflexion, knee extension, hip extension, and neutral pelvis. Running and walking mechanics are similar, except both feet are briefly off the ground when an individual is running.Compressive forces will also be present for the spine during running activities. Joints may go through flexion, extension, circumduction, abduction, adduction, or hyperextension for running, yoga, and resistance training.

Negative Effects When Training Is Ceased

When a client stops training for an extended period, muscles begin to atrophy and the cardiovascular and muscular systems become deconditioned. In addition, clients may notice aches and pains returning and their range of motion becomes more limited. They will lose the ability to complete tasks that require increased levels of coordination with an economy of energy and may become short of breath with a lower amount of exertion. When they resume training, clients can increase their abilities and functional performance within the cardiovascular and muscular systems. The rule of thumb is "if you don't use it, you lose it."

Overtraining

Overtraining can result from a desire to get in shape faster by exercising longer and harder than is necessary and not utilizing rest periods. It can also be the result of poor self-image or an eating disorder. It is necessary for the personal trainer to educate the client on the dangers of overtraining and how it can be avoided. The following are signs that the client may be overtraining:

- fatigue
- moodiness
- unenthusiastic about workouts
- difficulty sleeping at night
- irritation

If these signs are obvious in the client to a great extent, it may be necessary to refer the client to a physician.

Improper Form and Technique

Using improper technique and form during cardiovascular or resistance activities can be detrimental to a client's health. It can cause overuse or acute injuries, which impede a client's progress and prevent them from reaching health goals. Injury may cause a client to have misgivings about continuing an exercise routine and lower motivation to become healthy if the fear of injury is present. Improper technique lessens the benefit of the activity because the muscles are not trained appropriately. Inappropriate motor patterns for the movement are recorded in the client's mind, and they should "unlearn" the wrong technique to learn the right technique. It is always more beneficial to learn the correct technique the first time.

Performing movements with improper form can have long term consequences. It is important for the trainer to understand altered muscle lengths, synergistic dominance, and altered reciprocal. Reciprocal inhibition occurs when the muscles on one side of a joint relax while the muscles on the other side of the joint contract. Reciprocal inhibition helps to create coordinated movement during exercise. During a bicep curl, for instance, reciprocal inhibition is the way in which the biceps contract while the triceps lengthen. Altered reciprocal inhibition refers to an overactive or tight agonist muscle that stifles the proper function of its partner antagonist muscle—as with a tight hip flexor reciprocally inhibiting its antagonist muscle, the hip extensor. Synergistic dominance occurs when synergist muscles overcompensate for a weak prime mover muscle. This process is the body's backup system, allowing the muscles adjacent to the prime mover to pick up the slack when it is not functioning optimally. Synergistic dominance and altered reciprocal inhibition result in muscle imbalances that affect the kinetic chain. Synergistic dominance can occur because of an injured prime mover, an underdeveloped prime mover, or an overdeveloped secondary mover (synergist). An injury is likely once the synergist dominates because it was not designed to handle the load appropriately.

Appropriate Exercise Clothing

When exercising in outdoor conditions, the client must dress in weather appropriate clothing. If it is hot and humid outside, cotton is not an appropriate clothing choice because it does not wick away excess moisture from the skin. Synthetic materials that wick moisture from the body and breathe well are preferable. It is best to avoid wearing a hat, as that will also hold in heat. When exercising in a cold environment, the client must layer clothing and have a moisture-wicking layer closest to the skin. Layers of clothing should be removed as body temperature increases. The appropriate athletic shoe must also be chosen based on the activty performed. Referring a client to a reputable retailer that can help with fit is beneficial. A thinner-soled shoe is required for plyometric or resistance training, and is also more helpful for training in balance issues.

Learning Styles

It is important for the personal trainer to remember that each client has a unique learning style. The trainer should attempt to identify the client's learning style and tailor their teachings toward it. For instance, a kinesthetic learner may benefit from practicing the movement before actually beginning a set, as verbal instructions may be difficult to follow. A visual learner will learn best by watching the trainer go through a complete range of motion with the movement, and an auditory learner will rely heavily on verbal cues. Ideally, a trainer will provide verbal instruction, a physical demonstration, and guide the client through the movement to ensure that all three learning styles are covered.

Properly Spotting a Client

The principle of progressive overload suggests that the body only meets fitness goals when sufficiently challenged. It is important to challenge the body's limits to improve fitness, but there is an inherent injury risk associated with this practice. Spotting can significantly reduce this risk. When spotting, a trainer provides the client with a minimal amount of assistance to ensure they complete the repetition or set.

Spotting can occur anywhere within the range of motion. In the early stages of a lift, the trainer can provide assistance to ensure that the client can begin the movement safely. During the lift, the trainer can help the client through any difficult or "sticking" points. At the end of the lift, the trainer can help the client safely return the weight to the end position. When spotting, it is important to provide only as much assistance as the client needs. The trainer should not be performing the movement for the client. Before the exercise begins, the trainer should discuss what the spot. If a spot requires physical contact, the client should be made aware, and the trainer should obtain consent to make physical contact.

Monitoring Clients During Exercise

Determining Whether an Exercise Session Should End or Continue

Labored breathing, an inability to talk, a flushed face, or complaints of sharp pain are indications that a workout is too intense. If the client stops on his or her own, the personal trainer needs to assess whether the client can continue working out after a short break. If the client's heart rate lowers significantly and the client feels able to continue, exercise can continue. If the client still feels faint or exasperated following the break, the session may need to be terminated.

Normal and Abnormal Response to Exercise

In a healthy adult, the normal response to exercise is increased heart rate and blood pressure as blood is shuttled to the working muscles. In an adult with chronic health issues, heart rate and/or blood pressure may rise too quickly and cause negative symptoms that may cause the exercise session to be terminated. The personal trainer must make sure adults with chronic conditions begin exercising according to their appropriate protocols.

Improper Use of Cardiovascular Equipment

It is important to demonstrate and explain proper use of cardiovascular equipment to avoid injury. One example of improper technique when using cardiovascular equipment would be hunching over from the waist or gripping the bar on the treadmill. Both issues can cause poor posture and reduce the number of calories being used. Additionally, the client may become light-headed or dizzy because she is compressing her diaphragm by leaning over, which leads to insufficient breath intake and thus hyperventilation to get more air and oxygen to working muscles.

Improper Technique for Resistance Machines, Free Weights, and Stability Equipment

When training with resistance activity, form must be prioritized to avoid injury. In general, the client should perform movements with the feet under the hips, the hips under the shoulders, and the neck in a neutral position. Proper balance and range of motion are important. The proper technique should be explained and demonstrated before the client attempts the exercise and verbal cues should be provided during the exercise.With a resistance machine, any movement that causes the client to arch his back would be an example of improper technique and may indicate that he is using too much weight. For free weight exercises, if the client struggles to complete the move in general, or begins to lean backward to complete the movement, this is also improper technique. With stability equipment, any time it is used for something other than its intended purpose to promote balance, it is being used improperly.

Improper Stretching Techniques

Stretching is an important element of a successful training session, but proper form and technique are important. Failure to avoid common mistakes can cause injury. It is important to avoid stretching a cold muscle. A warmup consisting of light cardiovascular activity is ideal to prepare the body for stretching activities. An example of improper technique for partner stretching would be for the partner to force a muscle to stretch farther than it is capable of stretching due to muscle tightness or impaired range of motion. With static stretching, the client must be sure to hold the stretch rather than bouncing in the stretch, as this would promote muscle injury. With dynamic stretching, it would be improper for the client to move a joint outside of its normal range of motion to heighten the stretch.

Assessment of Client's Understanding

There are various ways for a personal trainer to assess the client's understanding of the movement patterns. Once the trainer has demonstrated the proper technique and provided verbal instructions to the client on how to do a specific exercise, they can ask if what was said makes sense. Additionally, they can ask if the client has any questions before beginning the exercise. Finally, it will become clear during the movement if the client has an understanding of the instructions and demonstration. If they perform the movement improperly, it is likely they lack clear understanding of the expectations.

Effective Communication of Proper Technique and Feedback

When providing feedback to a client regarding proper technique for exercise, the personal trainer should utilize as many avenues as possible to communicate. The trainer can verbally explain the proper technique. A demonstration of the movement pattern should follow the verbal instructions. The client should attempt the movement pattern without resistance. As the client is performing the movement, the personal trainer should provide verbal cues and spot the client to ensure the proper movement pattern is understood. Throughout the process, the client should be encouraged to ask questions. When providing feedback regarding client performance, the trainer should begin by praising what the client has done correctly and point out improvements made since the initial exercise testing. Additionally, once the trainer has given feedback to the client, the client should be allowed to ask questions. In areas where the client is still deficient in performance, the trainer should share a plan for improvement.

Modifying to Exercise Frequency, Intensity, Time, and Duration

Modification of Exercise Programs for Pregnant Women

Pregnant women should not perform exercise when absolute contraindications are present. Although this is true of any client, pregnant women prsent unique challenges that require special attention from the trainer. If any of the relative contraindications are present for a pregnant woman, modifications will be necessary to her typical routine. Additionally, as she progresses further into her pregnancy, her center of gravity shifts forward, requiring exercise to be modified for comfort. For adults, seniors, children, adolescents, and pregnant women, exercise may be modified for an acute injury or sickness, extreme discomfort associated with an exercise, or extreme temperatures. If a client is dehydrated, exercise should be stopped altogether.

Benefits of Modifications for Clients with Chronic Disease

When clients with chronic disease receive clearance to exercise, the exercises should be modified to accommodate the client's limitations. In the initial stages of an exercise routine, clients may need modifications to feel successful with what they are doing. As they progress through their workout plan and begin to meet their goals, exercises may have to be modified to become more challenging and, and the client may need to set new goals. Modifications provide a range of choices for clients so they can have autonomy over their workout routines. When designing a program for a client who is exercising under a doctor's orders, it is important to take their recent medical history into account and progress exercises accordingly. Heart rate and level of exertion (using the Borg RPE scale) should be monitored throughout the session.

Avoiding Training Plateaus

Specificity

Specificity of exercise refers to training that upholds a specific goal; for instance, strength training requires different protocol than speed training. The principle of specificity is frequently referred to by an alternate name, the specific adaptation to imposed demands (SAID) principle, which simply states that a person's body will learn to cope with added stresses placed on it. The take away from this principle is that the body will adapt to meet the demands that are placed on it. The trainer must design a program that challenges the client's body to adapt in the desired fashion.When training for strength, an example of specificity would be to create a particular goal for each session that focuses on strength for a certain area. One session might focus on core strength, while the next focuses on lower body strength. Specificity helps to avoid a training plateau because the personal trainer is keeping track of when the client reaches the training goals for strength in a particular area. Once this goal is reached, a new goal can be made, with the training sessions specifically corresponding to it.

Progressive Overload

The term progressive overload refers to progressively overloading a bodily system for exercise training. The Overload Principle states that each workout should place a demand on the muscle or muscles that is greater than that in the previous workout session. Overload can be achieved by increasing the resistance or weight, increasing repetitions, increasing sets, or decreasing the rest period between sets or exercises. For instance, one way of achieving progressive overload for cardiovascular endurance training would be to increase distance run by a half-mile per week. This helps the client to achieve the overall goal of a specific distance while also training the cardiovascular system to function more efficiently. However, since the distance is being increased, it keeps the body from becoming overly efficient and expending fewer calories at a distance that becomes too comfortable for training purposes.

Proper Progression of Exercise Sessions

To reach the client goals at all, the personal trainer must continue to pay attention to proper progression of exercise from simple to complex. There are a variety of ways to progress an exercise. Per ACSM, Progression is the systematic changes in exercise prescription (e .g., intensity, duration, frequency) necessary to increase fitness. Additionally, individual exercises can be made more challenging by adding instablity, increasing proprioceptic demand, or using imbalanced loads among other tactics. If training remains simple for the client, major cardiovascular and muscular gains will not be made. Additionally, a training plateau will occur once the body becomes overly efficient with an exercise routine. Changing one or more exercise variables (overload, specificity, duration, frequency) will allow the training plateau to be overcome.

Proper Progression for Developing Strength in Chest and Legs

A proper exercise progression goes from simple to complex, single-joint to multi-joint exercises. As an example, proper progression for strength development in the chest might be as follows: assisted bench press on a resistance machine, bench press with free weights and an exercise ball, push-ups, burpees. For strength progression in the legs, an example of a proper progression would be seated leg extension, seated leg press, squat, side shuffle to a squat. The personal trainer should spot the client at each point of the progression.

Periodized Training Program to Increase or Maintain Athletic Performance Variables

The ACSM describes progressive training as "the act of moving forward or advancing towards a specific goal over time until the target goal has been achieved." Progressive overload is defined as "the gradual increase in stress placed upon the body during exercise training." In other words, it is a systematic way of changing up a client's training routine, so his or her body does not plateau but continues to make progress toward fitness goals while avoiding overtraining and overuse injuries.

For example, the first period of training might be for strength and general cardiovascular fitness. The second period of training could be for speed and sport-specific skills with maintenance strength training. The third period of training could include the sports season, with maintenance for speed, strength, and sport-specific skills. The fourth period could include recovery, with limited endurance and strength training, while increasing exercise load towards the end of the period to prepare for the first period again.

Gaining Client Feedback

Feedback Regarding Client's Experience and Assessment of Progress

There are a variety of ways for a personal trainer to gain insight into how a client perceives their training. The trainer can ask the client if they feel like they are meeting their goals. The trainer can create a checklist or survey for the client to fill out when goals are reassessed. At the end of the training, the personal trainer can ask the client to fill out a satisfaction survey to indicate the overall success of the program from the client's perspective.

Reviewing Current Goals and Creating New Goals

The personal trainer should assess the client goals at frequent intervals throughout the exercise program. For instance, if the client has contracted to work with the personal trainer for 40 sessions, it might be good to assess some of the minor goals every 5 sessions, while assessing the primary goal(s) every 10 sessions. This gives enough time for change to take place, but the assessments are close enough together for the client to have the goals in mind during each workout. Once a goal is met, a new goal should take its place. The personal trainer and the client should both keep a log of when the goals are met and when new goals are created.

Leadership & Education Implementation

Applying Communication, Motivation, and Behavioral Strategies

Communication with Clients

There are various ways to communicate with a client, and the personal trainer must find out which type of communication the client responds to best. Talking with the client over the phone is most beneficial if the client can be reached easily via telephone, although the personal trainer needs to understand the protocol of the fitness center for making such calls from her personal number. Depending on the fitness facility, email and text reminders for appointments can be appropriate if done through a business email or contact number. The personal trainer needs to be careful about sending personal information regarding the client through these avenues. Additionally, keeping an updated newsletter or website can be a means of communicating mass information to several clients; however, some clients may not use these sources as a general rule.

Verbal and Nonverbal Communication

Communication throughout the exercise session is both verbal and nonverbal. The personal trainer should give verbal instructions and encouragement to the client while also realizing that body language will affect the client as well. It is important to make eye contact with the client and speak kindly and confidently, so the client understands that their time and effort are valued. The personal trainer should maintain a professional appearance at all times. The trainer should maintain a pleasant facial expression and focus their attention on the client throughout the session.

Active Listening

Active listening means that the personal trainer is listening to what the client has to say, looking at the client while she speaks, and asking questions at appropriate times to be sure of what the client means. Examples of active listening would be making eye contact with the client, jotting down notes regarding what the client is saying, repeating back what the client said to convey understanding ("So what I understand you to mean is..."), and making any necessary changes to the workout routine based on the client's feedback.

Auditory, Visual, and Kinesthetic Learning Styles

An auditory learner learns best through verbal instructions, a visual learner responds best to a visual demonstration or presentation, and a kinesthetic learner benefits from trying something to understand it better. Typically, clients will benefit when the information is presented with a blend of styles. One way to ensure the client understands what is needed for a movement pattern is to describe the movement, model the movement for the client, then have the client complete a practice movement without any weight or through a partial range of motion if the movement requires body weight as resistance.

Feedback

Feedback can be given to a client in a variety of ways. Evaluative feedback helps the client know what she is doing correctly and incorrectly in the movement pattern ("You are doing a great job of not allowing your knees to go past your toes, but make sure your toes are pointed forward."). Supportive feedback is a means of encouraging the client, perhaps through a difficult part of the workout ("I know it's tough, but we're almost through. Do you think you can finish 2 more laps?"). Descriptive feedback is clear and concise feedback that provides correction at the end of a movement pattern or session ("In future squat-type exercises, I want you to focus on squeezing the muscles of your gluteus to decrease pressure on your knees."). Feedback should be given to the client verbally at regular intervals, but also in written form when she is regularly evaluated for goal assessment.

Behavior Change Models

There are several different behavior change models, for instance, socio-ecological model, readiness to change model, social cognitive theory, and theory of planned behavior. With the socio-ecological model, the personal trainer understands that there are several different influences—personal characteristics, interpersonal relationships, community relationships, and societal influence—that combine to determine a person's pattern of behavior. The social cognitive theory proposes that personal characteristics, environmental characteristics, and behavior are interconnected and influence one another. The readiness to change model states that someone will pass through certain stages—precontemplation, contemplation, preparation, action, and maintenance—on the journey to change a behavior. The theory of planned behavior states that subjective norms, behavioral beliefs, and perceived behavior control all work together to cause some to have an intention to modify behavior.

When the personal trainer understands the client's motivation, they can more effectively help clients reach their goals. For instance, a client comes to a personal trainer and expresses in the initial evaluation that she has been amazed at the high rates of diabetes in the United States and so has decided to have her physical for the first time in several years. Upon having her physical, she found her blood sugar levels to be uncharacteristically high and thus decided she needed to lose some weight. The client realized she needed some assistance in reaching her goal and called a personal trainer. In this example, personal characteristics and societal influences worked together to cause the client to modify behavior (socio-ecological model). Additionally, the client can be categorized as being in the preparation step of the readiness to change model. Finally, a problem in society caused the client to become conscious of their health (subjective norms), assess their health, and determine it needed to change (behavioral beliefs and perceived behavior control).

Interference with Client Faithfulness to Exercise Programming

There are a variety of factors that can limit a client's faithfulness to their exercise program. The trainer should recognize that adherence is faltering, identify what is causing the motivation to wane, and get the client back on track. Poor attendance, waning enthusiasm for workouts, and disinterest are signs that adherence is waning. There are many potential causes, asking a few probing questions is an excellent way to identify what may be causing the change. If there is extra stress in a client's personal life, he may be less inclined to follow through with appointments. Work schedule and finances can also cause unfaithfulness to exercise. Falling back into poor nutritional habits and the guilt associated with poor diet choices can lead to canceled training sessions. If a client feels that the personal trainer is not an effective communicator, or is not listening to him, he may express reluctance in moving forward with more sessions. Sometimes clients may fear not getting the results they want to see for themselves, may not manage their time wisely, or may not understand how to implement changes at home that will help them in their training sessions. It is the trainer's job to stay positive and help coach clients through these issues.

Influencing a Client to Avoid Detrimental Behaviors

Avoiding potential obstacles is a key to client success. Identifying the potential pitfalls before starting a training program and discussing them with the client is perhaps the most effective method of avoiding detrimental behaviors. A personal trainer can help a client avoid many of the pitfalls associated with outside stressors or relapses into previous poor habits by creating an "open door policy." The trainer can encourage honesty from the client while offering encouragement and constructive advice for avoiding common pitfalls. It is necessary for the trainer to provide compassionate accountability for clients who may be more prone to fall back into sedentary habits. A trainer has to hold their clients accountable. This means setting goals together, making sure the client is diligently following their program, and providing constructive criticism when necessary. It is important to demonstrate compassion for the client while holding them accountable. Understanding the struggles the client is facing, and caring about them as an individual will build rapport, and result in better results. In short, the trainer does not have to be a drill sergeant type to help their client achieve results. Being firm but fair is a better approach.

Increasing Client Motivation to Achieve Fitness Goals

Personal trainers can help clients reach fitness goals by working patiently with them, reminding them of their progress, and showing them objectively how they are reaching their goals. Serving as a motivator is one of a trainer's most important functions. The best training plan in the world is useless, if the client cannot summon the motivation to participate. Reaching a fitness goal can be a daunting task, but an inspirational trainer can make the prospect of achieving a goal seem more plausible. Reaching fitness goals requires consistency, and a motivated client is more likely to train consistently. Offering encouragement, being supportive, and demonstrating a positive attitude are excellent motivational tactics that a trainer can employ. Trainers can also motivate clients by rewarding them for reaching their goals. Trainers can encourage clients to identify who can be a part of their social support network. Understanding how to motivate clients will enable the clients to be more faithful in reaching their goals.

Extrinsic and Intrinsic Reinforcement Strategies

Extrinsic or external rewards are the positive outcomes received from others. An extrinsic reinforcement strategy is an external way of rewarding or reinforcing positive client behavior. For example, if a client has recently reached a goal of losing 5 lbs, the trainer can positively reinforce and reward the client reaching the goal by giving her the opportunity to engage in only her favorite fitness activities for one session. Intrinsic rewards are the benefits gained because of the rewarding nature of the activity. An intrinsic reward or reinforcement would increase self-esteem; using the same example, if a client lost 5 lbs, her intrinsic reinforcement would be the increase in self-esteem.

Helping Clients Increase Physical Activity Outside of Exercise Sessions

It is important for the client to understand the need to increase energy expenditure throughout the day in addition to the structured exercise sessions. The trainer must avoid assuming that this is common knowledge and educate the client. It is important to provide examples of activities that increase energy expenditure and offer advice to the client on how to be more active. The personal trainer can help by having the client describe a typical daily routine and then make suggestions on how to increase levels of activity. For example, the personal trainer might suggest the client take the stairs to the office instead of the elevator, park a little farther from the office entrance than normal, or take 5 minutes every hour of work to walk around the office a few times.

Healthy Lifestyle

Phyisical fitness is one element of a healthy lifestyle. Although "healthy lifestyle" is a broad term, there are several factors that can be safely considered an integral part of healthy living. Engaguing in physical activity, consuming a a balanced diet, caring for one's phyiscal and mental health, refraining from consuming drugs, and avoiding dangerous activities are lifestyle choices that promote health. The personal trainer is instrumental in helping the client understand what options are available for a healthy lifestyle. The personal trainer can take time at each session to discuss with the client the choices he has made throughout the week and how he can be more effective by choosing healthier options. The personal trainer becomes a mentor, source of accountability, cheerleader, and coach for the client and must encourage honest communication so the client can receive the best results of his programming.

LIFESTYLE MANAGEMENT TECHNIQUES AND HEALTH COACHING PRINCIPLES

It is difficult (and perhaps impossible) to adhere to a fitness program if one's life is in disarray. It is important for the trainer to help a client manage their life, stress, and health. Offering advice and helping the client techniques to better manage their lives will increase the likelihood that the client reaches their fitness goals. One example of a lifestyle management technique is to have the client keep a food log and an activity log each week. The trainer can take the logs, make suggestions, and return the logs to the client to help promote change. Another example is to help the client identify sources of stress in her life and help create alternatives for managing it. Anytime the client can help in creating solutions to issues that stand in the way of well-being and health, the more likely she will be to follow through on the course of action.

AGE- AND FITNESS-APPROPRIATE LEVELS OF FITNESS EDUCATION

Fitness education is important for client success, and the onus is on the trainer to educate the client. The personal trainer needs to identify how clients receive information best, and attempt to present their education using the client's preferred method. For instance, if some clients do not like to read, then giving them helpful articles might not be the best course of action. It is best to provide a variety of resources and opportunities for clients to learn more about fitness. For instance, newsletters, articles, short instructional videos, and verbal teaching can all be effective for client learning. Additionally, if there are some hands-on learning opportunities during the training session, this may work best for some clients. The trainer should be sensitive to any possible learning barriers clients may have and try to work around that. The more clients understand the whys and hows of the benefits of fitness, the more likely they are to stick with their program. The trainer must remember that fitness education is ongoing and not a one-time occurrence. Fitness is a lifestyle. Clients who are knowledgable about fitness and empowered to make healthy lifestyle choices will enjoy more long-term success than those who lack fitness knowledge.

Educating Clients

Influence of Lifestyle Factors on Lipid and Lipoprotein Levels

A sedentary lifestyle, poor nutrition, and high stress levels are the most influential factors that cause unhealthy lipid levels for clients. When clients begin a normal exercise routine, begin to make healthy food choices, and learn to manage their stress more effectively, they notice a difference in their lipid levels. Genetics can play a role in predisposing a client to have high lipid profiles, but it takes unhealthy lifestyle choices to cause their genes to create poor health.

Body Composition, Body Mass Index, and Lean Body Mass

Body composition refers to the ratio of lean body mass (or fat-free mass) to fat mass in a client. Body mass index is one way of assessing this ratio and relies on height and weight information to do so. BMI is an acronym that stands for body mass index. BMI is inexact. It is a simple method to determine if a client's weight is proportional to their height. BMI indicates general health risks but is not a reliable indicator of fitness level. A muscular individual will have a high BMI without the health risks associated with a high BMI. A lean marathon runner may have a low BMI but is still fit. The Quetelet index is another name for BMI. BMI does not measure body fat, but it is a useful assessment tool to determine whether a person's weight correlates in a healthy manner to his or her height. Use the following formula to determine BMI:

$$\text{BMI} = \frac{\text{Weight (in kilograms)}}{\text{Height}^2 \text{ (in meters}^2\text{)}}$$

BMI	Interpretation
Less than 18.5	Underweight
18.5-24.9	Normal
25-29.9	Overweight
30 or more	Obese

Typical Fat Distribution Patterns in Males and Females

Women tend to have a higher fat percentage than men do. Women tend to carry more fat in their hips and thighs (gynoid or pear shape) than men. Men tend to carry more fat in their midsection (android or apple shape) than women do. Briefly speaking, epinephrine is the hormone that stimulates the body to break down fat (lipolysis) for usable energy. Epinephrine stimulates lipolysis through beta receptors and inhibits it through alpha receptors; both of these receptor sites can be located on the same cell, but the epinephrine stimulates the receptor that has more locations. Abdominal adipocytes are more sensitive to beta receptor activation by epinephrine than are adipocytes in the hips and thighs and are easier to break down. Women especially tend to have more alpha receptors in the hips and thighs, which promote adipocyte storage.

Anorexia Nervosa and Bulimia Nervosa

Anorexia nervosa and bulimia nervosa are both eating disorders that arise from a client's distorted self-image. Characteristics of anorexia include severe body image disorder, heightened fear of becoming fat, and excessive restriction of calories. Symptoms that can be observed in a client include the following: severe weight loss, strict dietary practices, and heavy exercise participation. Bulimia is characterized by eating excessive amounts of food (often in secret) followed by vomiting and possibly the heavy use of diet pills or laxatives. Persons who binge eat may still be overweight, feel that they cannot control their eating, have a long (failed) history of dieting, and are not happy with their bodies. Either of these diseases can result in hospitalization, suicide, and impaired relationships with others. If a personal trainer suspects these conditions, the trainer should discuss it with the client (or guardian if under 18) and highly recommend counseling.

Body Composition and Overall Health

If a client is classified as overweight or obese, it can be an indicator of other health issues. In comparing body fat percentages in men, 3–5% body fat is essential for life, 6–10.9% is considered lean, 11–15.9% is considered fit, 16–19.9% is considered healthy, 20–24.9% is considered overweight and moderate risk for disease, and >25% is considered obese and high risk for disease. Likewise for women, 11–14.9% is considered essential for life, 15–18.9% is considered lean, 19–22.9% is considered fit, 23–26.9% is considered healthy, 27–31.9% is overweight and considered moderate risk for disease, and >32% is obese and considered high risk for disease. Waist-to-hip ratio is another easy way to classify the client's overall health in the field and to evaluate the current disease risk level. To find a person's waist-to-hip ratio, measure the smallest part of his or her waist and largest part of his or her hips. Divide the waist measurement by the hip measurement. Women whose ratio exceeds 0.80 are at risk of having obesity-related health problems. The same is true for men with ratios greater than 0.95.

Health Classification by Body Fat

Classification	Men	Women
Essential for life	3-5%	11–14.9%
Lean	6–10.9%	15–18.9%
Fit	11–15.9%	19–22.9%
Healthy	16–19.9%	23–26.9%
Overweight (moderate risk for disease)	20–24.9%	27–31.9%
Obese (high risk for disease)	>25%	>32%

Effects of Diet, Exercise, and Behavior Modification on Body Composition

Diet, exercise, and lifestyle affect a client's body composition, and body composition affects health. A healthy diet involves eating a diet high in fruits and vegetables, low in simple carbohydrates, and healthy amounts of protein and fats. A healthy individual should have a goal of exercising the recommended 150 minutes per week. An active lifestyle and effectively managing and reducing stress levels are essential to good health. Following these guidelines helps the body reduce fat storage, increases the effectiveness of the heart and circulation, and promotes a host of other positive changes. It is dangerous for clients to think their health can be changed by focusing on one or two of the variables. It is crucial for the client to seek positive changes in all three areas. Seeking change in only one or two areas will result in positive changes to occur slowly, or not at all. Clients will also be more likely to engage in unsafe practices; for instance, if they are only trying to modify their exercise habits without modifying their nutritional or stress habits, they may over exercise to unsafe levels to try to achieve their goal.

Hydration

Water

Water is composed of two hydrogen molecules and one oxygen molecule (H2O). Water is one of the most abundant compounds on the planet and makes up almost two-thirds of the human body. Because it is used for many purposes (e.g., cooling the body off and removing waste from the body) and excreted, it must be regularly replaced to avoid dehydration. While nutritional deficiencies can take a long time to become a problem, humans cannot live for very long without ingesting clean water, or they will suffer serious, and potentially fatal effects. Basic body functions are impacted if a person loses as little as 2 percent of his or her total weight in water.

Benefits of adequate hydration include adequate blood levels, consistent body temperature, optimally functioning hormonal systems, and preventing edema, or water retention.

Training and Sports Activities

Water and fluids are essential to fitness training. The body is composed largely of water and needs a continual replenishment to function properly. Exercise and fitness activities hasten the loss of fluids, primarily through perspiration, and require a person to replace lost fluid to maintain performance capabilities.

Dehydration is associated with lower blood volume, lower blood pressure, heightened heart rate, and sodium retention, which in turn lead to fluid retention.

A person's weight can be used as a starting point to determine how much liquid is needed. An individual's weight upon waking in the morning can be considered 0. Before exercising or beginning any strenuous fitness activity; a person should ingest enough liquids to put his or her weight back to the 0 mark.

Guidelines for Hydration

A few hours before any exercise, the client should drink 16 ounces of fluids and consume up to twice that amount if it is hot out. During exercise, the client should replenish each hour with 20 to 40 ounces of fluids. After exercising, the client should weigh him- or herself and assess how many pounds off the 0 mark he or she is; the client should then drink 20 ounces per pound lost, especially if he or she is in heavy training or is an endurance athlete.

If the client is having a regular training session and the exercising will last approximately an hour, water will be the best choice for rehydration. If the client plans to train for more than an hour, Gatorade or a similar drink will be most beneficial. To stimulate faster stomach emptying, encourage the drinking of cold beverages.

Proper Nutritional and Portion Guidance

If a client is seeking help about establishing better nutritional habits and portion control, the personal trainer should be ready to provide resources. Personal trainers should provide general nutritional guidelines and provide information on healthy eating habits. The personal trainer should not prescribe specific diets. The client should be referred to a licensed dietician for specific diet plans. Some resources include ACSM dietary guidelines as found on their website, www.choosemyplate.gov, and websites where clients can gain access to guidance on healthy meals they can make. Additionally, if a client eats out frequently, the personal trainer can show the client how to navigate a restaurant website to find the healthiest option and how to have a backup plan for unexpected times of eating out.

At its core, Choose My Plate is a plan for how much of a person's total diet each category of food should contribute. The United States Department of Agriculture, the creator of Choose My Plate, also recommends limiting foods with saturated fats, trans fats, added sugars, and sodium.

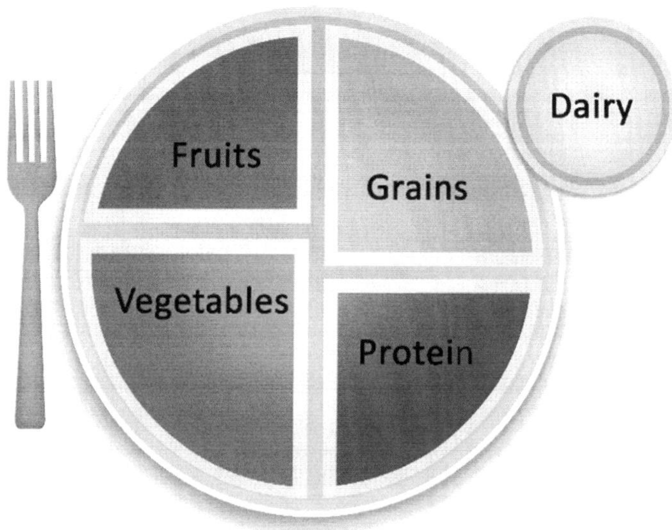

Female Athlete Triad

The female athlete triad is comprised of the following three elements: disordered eating, osteoporosis, and amenorrhea. Disordered eating leads to low levels of energy, osteoporosis leads to bone loss, and amenorrhea can lead to low iron levels or anemia. If a female has low iron levels or anemia, she doesn't have an effective way to make use of oxygen for energy because ultimately, hemoglobin production will be low and oxygen binds to hemoglobin. If she doesn't have enough hemoglobin production, she will not utilize oxygen appropriately for energy production. If bone loss occurs, females will be more likely to fracture or break bones and sprain or strain joints, ligaments, and tendons. If a female has low energy, she will not be able to put in or get out of her workouts the quality that is necessary for reaching her goals. Overall, if a female athlete suffers from the triad, her performance is hindered, and her health is put in jeopardy.

Inappropriate Weight Loss Techniques

Clients who have been sedentary for a long time may attempt to lose weight more quickly than what is healthy for them. They may over-exercise, buy into fad diets, go on a completely liquid diet, take dietary supplements that are unsafe or interact negatively with other medications that they may be taking, or they may engage in anorexic or bulimic behaviors in an attempt to lose weight more quickly. Fad diets are often based on unsound scientific evidence or pseudoscience. Fad diets often result in water or muscle weight loss rather than fat loss. Liquid diets often result in severely reduced calorie consumption that can lead to malnourishment and inadequate fuel to support bodily systems. As an industry, dietary supplements are not always regulated, and clients may not be getting exactly what they think they are with their supplements. Medicine and food face intense scrutiny and regulation by the FDA. The FDA does not regulate supplements, and their claims are often unfounded. With anorexic or bulimic behavior, clients may either severely restrict calories (anorexia) or binge and purge (bulimia), which greatly harms their overall health. The desire in these situations is to achieve a certain weight loss despite health risks that may be present. The trainer should always encourage healthy weight loss and set realistic weight loss goals for the client.

If a personal trainer suspects a client is engaging in unhealthy weight loss techniques, the trainer must attempt to educate the client on why those behaviors are ultimately harmful to the overall goal of weight loss. The client needs to understand that it takes time to put the weight on, and it will take time to take the weight off. Because of the law of thermodynamics (calories consumed vs. calories burned) and the fact that a pound of fat contains 3500 calories, weight loss exceeding 1-3 pounds a weak is not sustainable or healthy. They also need to have expectations that are reasonable for their age and abilities; if the client is older, it is not reasonable to expect he will look like they did in his teenage years.

Kilocalorie Content of Fat, Protein, Carbohydrate, and Alcohol

Proteins act as a building block for new or damaged body tissues. Proteins are a viable energy source and are required by the body to synthesize other necessary nutrients.

Proteins are composed of amino acids. There are three different categories of amino acids: essential (meaning the body cannot create them itself), semi-essential (meaning elements can be made by the body, but other parts need an external source), and nonessential (meaning the body can create them from other sources).

The essential amino acids have to be ingested from a direct source. The nonessential amino acids can be pieced together by the body from nitrogen and other source material (lipids and carbohydrates).

Essential amino acids	Semi-essential amino acids	Nonessential amino acids
Histidine	Arginine	Alanine
Isoleucine	Cysteine	Asparagine
Leucine	Glutamine	Aspartic acid
Lysine	Glycine	Glutamic acid
Methionine	Proline	Serine
Phenylalanine	Tyrosine	
Threonine		
Tryptophan		
Valine		

Digestion and Use of Proteins

Proteins are made up of chains of amino acids held together by peptides. For the body to be able to use these amino acids, the entire protein chain has to be broken down into its individual amino acids. This begins when the proteins come into contact with the hydrochloric acid in the stomach, and it continues as the proteins enter the large and small intestines.

Proteins can then be used in different ways, depending on what the body needs at that time. A protein can do three main things once released into the blood via the liver. It can be used immediately as energy, be stored as fat, or be used to build or repair body tissues.

Foods That Contain Proteins

A variety of foods contain proteins. Food that comes from animals (e.g., animal meat, eggs, milk, and dairy products) contains substantial amounts of protein. Food that contains all of the essential amino acids is called a complete protein. If it only has some of the essential amino acids, it is called an incomplete protein (such as peanut butter).

The amino acid that is missing or only present in trace amounts is the limiting factor. A complete protein must be synthesized. The missing protein determines (limits) the amount of protein that can be made. Think of a spice recipe that calls for 2 cups of salt, pepper, and garlic. If the chef only has 1 cup of garlic, the spice mix cannot be made, and the garlic is said to be the limiting factor.

Vegetarians eat only certain types of protein, which may be incomplete or have a low limiting factor. Vegetarians should work with a nutritionist who specializes in vegan or vegetarian diets to ensure they eat enough complete protein sources.

Complete Protein Profiles

Protein is evaluated on how well it functions as a complete nutrient, and if it provides all of the essential amino acids in the ratios needed for consumption.

Biologic value (BV) is a popular term used to describe how much a given protein satisfies the needed amino acid values. It is a common catchphrase used in fitness circles and vitamin supplement advertising. The higher the BV of the protein, the more closely it supplies all the needed amino acids.

Net protein utilization (NPU) and protein efficiency ratio (PER) are two terms that mean the same thing: how well a given protein meets the needs of the human body.

Amounts of Proteins

The amount of protein that an individual needs to consume will depend on various factors such as height, weight, activity level, and activity level. For example, if a person does intense aerobic and anaerobic exercises, his or her protein requirements may be higher.

Most of a person's basic energy needs should be met with carbohydrates and lipids, with protein used for tissue repair and as a backup energy source, unless the client is a competitive weight lifter.

If a person consumes high-quality protein sources, less of it will be needed. If the protein sources are less complete, with a lower BV, more protein will be needed to provide all the essential amino acids.

Negative Energy Balance

A negative energy balance (achieved by burning more calories than are consumed) is required if a client wants to lose weight or reduce body fat percentage. When this state is achieved, the body uses amino acids to generate energy in a process called gluconeogenesis. Protein is required to fuel this process.

Clients who reduce overall calorie intake and increase activity levels will require an increase in lean protein consumption. Protein will be used for energy, to repair tissues from exercise, and to help prevent the loss of muscle mass that often accompanies a weight-loss regimen.

Protein Needs

Because protein acts as a building block for body tissues, persons interested in hypertrophy, particularly weight-lifting clients seeking maximal hypertrophy for competitive bodybuilding purposes, will need to ingest much more protein than the average healthy adult. This will also help taper body fat down to very low ratios, a necessity during the competition season.

However, this should be used as a temporary diet strictly for use during competition times. Because the body's protein needs will be higher because of the specific training, protein will be upped dramatically while overall calories from other sources will be reduced. Consuming a high-protein diet on a long-term basis is not recommended, and keeping body fat to single-digit percentages is not healthy beyond this purpose.

By cycling back to a regular diet when not competing, the bodybuilding client will be able to achieve better muscle mass when competing in the future than he or she would if the high-protein diet was constantly employed.

SATIETY

A feeling of fullness (satiety) after eating is important for several reasons. First, it gives a signal to stop ingesting more calories at that sitting. It also signals to the body that calories have been consumed, something that may not be triggered when a person drinks the same number of calories in a beverage or shake form. Protein also takes longer to process, leading to feeling full for a longer period, with steadier energy levels throughout the day.

Protein is more satisfying than other nutrients, specifically lipids (fats) and carbohydrates. Animal studies have shown that when the animals are given protein, they can go longer until the next feeding than when given fat or carbohydrates alone. This indicates that protein satisfies hunger for a longer period and provides more satiety.

RDA OF PROTEIN

An average healthy person should aim to ingest 0.8 grams of protein for every kilogram of body weight (approximately 30 percent of daily calorie intake).

Those who are engaged in fitness or training activities should ingest more protein to help with tissue repair and muscle building. For a person who works out regularly, this would include a minimum of 1 gram of protein for every kilogram of body weight and somewhere around 1.5 grams of protein for every kilogram of body weight when doing muscle-building activities.

For an endurance athlete, 1.4 grams of protein for every kilogram of body weight is needed during regular training, bumped up to as much as 2 grams per kilogram of body weight during competition training.

Competitive weight lifters would need 1 gram of protein for every kilogram of body weight during noncompetitive periods and jump up to somewhere around 2 grams per kilogram of body weight during competitive training times.

Normal activity Level	Recommended daily protein intake
Sedentary	0.8 g/kg (0.4 g/lb.)
Strength athlete	1.2–1.7 g/kg (0.5–0.8 g/lb.)
Endurance athlete	1.2–1.4 g/kg (0.5–0.6 g/lb.)

PROTEIN-BASED DIET DRAWBACKS

High-protein diets have enjoyed popularity in the last decade, touting weight loss benefits. However, research shows that high protein diets are not the best dietary choice for people. High-protein diets tend to include higher levels of bad fats and reduce ingestion of dietary fiber, which can lead to a higher risk of serious diseases.

High-protein diets require much more water to digest properly, raising the risk that a person can become dehydrated more easily.

Another serious problem associated with high-protein diets is potential calcium loss. When people eat more protein than they need, their bodies lose calcium.

High-protein diets also force the body into ketosis (a state where the body uses fat as its main source of energy), which many doctors and nutritionists feel is unsafe on a long-term basis.

Extra Protein

There is no scientific evidence to prove that consuming extra protein in the form of supplements gives a uniform result to overall fitness gains or muscle hypertrophy. However, when a person is working out, his or her protein needs may go up to supply the body with building blocks to build and repair tissues and as a backup fuel source.

Ingesting protein after a workout has been shown to increase important endocrine activities that may support muscle building, rather than straight repair.

Supplements can also be used when a client is trying to lose body fat by acting as a replacement, giving needed protein while avoiding excess calories. Supplements can be consumed very quickly and easily in the form of portable shakes or bars, ensuring that a client ingests needed fuel before a workout.

Supplemental Protein

Many supplement manufacturers attempt to create a perfect protein that can be used by the body better than actual food sources or other supplements. The perfect protein would assimilate quickly and contain the perfect balance of amino acids.

A popular trend in supplemental protein is whey protein, which can be found in a variety of supplements. Whey protein has the best biologic value of all supplemental proteins and has been shown in studies to provide greater benefits than other kinds of protein.

It is debatable if extra protein is necessary, even for active individuals. Whey protein supplements are appropriate for competitive weight lifters in competition mode; these athletes have high protein needs and are seeking to reduce overall calories.

Carbohydrates

Carbohydrates are made up of three basic elements: oxygen, hydrogen, and carbon. Carbohydrates are macronutrients that fall into three categories:

- Fiber
- Simple carbohydrates (sugar)
- Complex carbohydrates (starch)

Sugars can further be classified as mono- or disaccharides—having one or two sugar units. Fructose (plant sugar) and glucose (blood sugar) are common monosaccharides. Lactose (milk sugar) and sucrose (table sugar) are common disaccharides.

Carbohydrates are the body's main supply of energy and have other wide-ranging functions, including playing a part in the digestion of other micronutrients.

Digestion and Use

The body digests different forms of carbohydrates differently. Simple sugars are easily assimilated with little work by the body. These types of sugars are found in various fruits as well as honey.

Starches take more work to break down because of their double bond. Grains, potatoes, rice, and table sugar fall into this category and require more effort for the body to process.

Fiber in the form of cellulose, the fibrous element of many fruits and vegetables, cannot be completely broken down by the body. Roughage (undigested fiber) is extremely important to healthy intestinal function because it helps clean out the digestive tract and regulate bowel movements.

GI

The glycemic index (GI) measures how much a given micronutrient affects a person's blood sugar level and the body's insulin response. The test is simple: The measurement is made when a single food is eaten after a fasting period. The blood sugar is measured before and after the food is eaten to gauge the change in blood sugar level.

Eating different foods in combination may change the effect on blood sugar entirely.

Some diets tout the benefits of eating only foods that have a low GI score, claiming that foods with high GI scores will lead to negative effects, such as increased weight and fat gain. These diets tend to clump foods into positive and negative categories, ignoring the basic premise of energy balance (weight gain is the result of more calories taken in than are expended).

The concept of good versus bad foods is a bit misguided, though foods with a low GI score do tend to be very healthy for the diet.

Foods Across the Glycemic Index

The highest level on the GI chart is pure glucose (commonly known as blood sugar), which is immediately assimilated by the body and causes blood sugar to spike.

The next highest range includes honey, cooked potatoes without skins, and carrots. These are followed (in descending order) by whole wheat bread, cooked potatoes with the skins on, and rice; white bread and bananas; sucrose (table sugar) and corn; pasta, oatmeal, and oranges; dairy products and apples; fruit sugar (fructose) and legumes (such as beans); lowest on the GI scale are soybeans and legumes (such as peanuts).

Glycemic Index Classifications

GI #	Classification
>70	High
56–69	Moderate
<55	Low

Fiber

Fiber is an extremely important part of a healthy diet for many reasons. Fiber consists of indigestible cellulose or plant matter that travels through the digestive tract in its original form. Benefits of fiber include:

- Helps keep blood sugar levels even and manageable
- Helps keep a person regular and avoid constipation
- Helps avoid appendicitis
- Helps maintain a healthy bacteria balance
- Helps a person feel more full
- Helps prevent diverticulitis, an infection of the intestines
- Helps lower bad (LDL) cholesterol levels

Diets high in fiber are linked to lower risk factors for diseases such as some cancers and cardiac-related disorders (heart disease).

Athletic Ability

Carbohydrates are essential for fitness and sports performance because they provide the body with the most accessible source of energy, especially for anaerobic exercises or activities. (These would be categorized as quick, high-impact activities, typical of most sporting activities.) During long-term activities, the body relies on stored glycogen first and then on fat.

The phrase "Fat burns in a carbohydrate flame" has a specific meaning in the context of training. There must be sufficient carbohydrates available to keep the body's energy cycle even and continually burning fat, which maximizes fat loss. If there are not enough carbohydrates, muscle glycogen will be depleted, and performance will suffer. This can happen even when sufficient oxygen is circulating in the body.

Recommended Grams of Carbohydrates

For endurance athletes, carbohydrates are essential. There must be sufficient carbohydrates available to keep the body's energy cycle even without relying on muscle glycogen stores, which are finite. If there are not enough carbohydrates, muscle glycogen will be depleted, and performance will suffer. This can happen even when sufficient oxygen is circulating in the body.

Endurance athletes need high-carbohydrate diets. Carbohydrates should comprise about two-thirds of calories consumed, or somewhere between 5 and 10 grams of carbohydrate per kilogram of body weight. Complex carbohydrates are the best choice because of the variety of other nutrients and vitamins available in these food sources.

Because a person should not exercise on a full stomach, it is a good idea for him or her to eat several hours before a workout. The meal should include an ample supply of carbohydrates sufficient to build up glycogen stores before exercise. Research has shown that people who eat a solid carbohydrate source four hours before exercising get a noticeable improvement in performance for that workout, well over ten percent.

Eating before a morning workout is very important because energy stores will be depleted after a long sleep. If a full meal is not practical, an energy shake or fitness bar will suffice, so the stomach is not full, and the body can quickly process the fuel.

Carbohydrate Loading

Carbo-loading is a system of ingesting large quantities of carbohydrates before an endurance activity that will last more than an hour and a half. This is common for people who run long distances, such as marathoners. This is done because this activity uses a high percentage of the body's stores of glycogen. If there is insufficient carbohydrate available and the glycogen stores are used up, a bottoming-out effect can occur. By carbo-loading, the body can reinforce its glycogen stores, doubling its available energy stores.

A carbo-loading diet typically occurs over several days. First comes four days of lowering glycogen stores by eating few carbohydrates and engaging in heavy exercise activities. Then, the person recuperates for three days and ingests up to 10 grams of carbohydrates for each kilogram of body weight.

Traditional carbo-loading consisted of four days of exhaustive exercise and limited carbohydrates followed by three days of recuperation and maximal carbohydrate intake. This method can be hard on the body by adding extra stressors right before an endurance event, which can lead to increased injury risk and cause blood sugar levels to slip too low, causing fatigue and crankiness.

An alternate carbo-loading routine, aimed at increasing the body's stores of glycogen, was formulated in the early 1980s. The client ingests four grams of carbohydrate for every kilogram of body weight on the sixth, fifth, and fourth days before an endurance event. High-intensity exercise is also engaged in for a half hour on the sixth day and for three-quarters of an hour for the fifth and fourth days.

On the third and second days prior, high-intensity exercise is engaged in for only 20 minutes. However, 10 grams of carbohydrates for every kilogram of body weight are ingested. The day before the event entails no workout, but it does include the elevated carbohydrate count.

If a client is going to be doing more than an hour of intense exercise, ingesting carbohydrates during the training session may be advisable. This would help keep available energy in a reasonable range, prevent an exhaustion of glycogen stores from muscle tissue, and increase endurance and performance for up to an additional hour.

If the exercise or training requires endurance, hourly intake of carbohydrates is a necessity. The best method would be through sports beverages; these not only replace lost fluids, but they also give a balanced stream of carbohydrates to the body without filling the stomach with the bulk that accompanies solid food consumption. Experts recommend drinking from 20 to 40 fluid ounces of liquid with around a 5-percent carbohydrate solution.

Ingesting carbohydrates after working out can have several benefits: It helps the body replenish glycogen stores that were depleted in training; ingesting carbohydrates after exercise also helps the body repair itself after strenuous workouts.

It is important that carbohydrates be ingested quickly after exercising to maximize benefits. It is advisable to consume between 1 to 2 grams of carbohydrates for every kilogram of body weight within 30 minutes of completing a workout.

Research has shown that waiting two hours to ingest carbohydrates can have a serious negative impact on glycogen replenishment. This could be because the body is more receptive after the rigors of working out, due to its systems working at a higher performance level and the blood rapidly circulating.

Percentage of Diet

If a person is looking to lose fat and gain lean muscle, carbohydrates should be the most plentiful aspect of the diet, comprising at least half to three-quarters of all calories consumed. The person can further maximize the benefits of that carbohydrate intake by ingesting a good deal of dietary fiber in that 50 to 75 percent.

This advice is contrary to many popular fad diets, which continue to assert that carbohydrates are a dieter's enemy and contribute significantly to fat gain or the body's inability to lose fat. This is based on junk science. The more reasoned and accepted point of view is that a diet must consist of a higher percentage of carbohydrates to prevent the body from sapping muscle glycogen stores for energy, which then strips lean muscle. Water loss associated with this process can account for apparent weight loss, but it does little in the way of altering body composition.

Weight Gain

There is an ongoing claim that carbohydrates contribute to the increase in obesity in the United States. Because the fitness industry and the diet and supplements industry are so powerful, a substantial amount of time and scientific research has been devoted to proving that carbohydrate consumption leads to weight gain.

Research indicates that even though Americans ate a higher percentage of carbohydrates and less fat at the turn of the twentieth century, obesity was far less widespread than it is today. This is due to two simple factors: Modern people are less active and ingest far more overall calories than did their ancestors.

This supports the basic theory that body composition, weight gain, and obesity are not related to high carbohydrate intake as much as to energy imbalance (more calories consumed than burned).

Lipids

A lipid is a macronutrient that can be used by the body for various functions and includes oils, fatty substances, sterols, and phospholipids. Lipids in foods are usually either oil or fat, which are also called triglycerides. This is also the form that lipids are stored in the human body.

Lipids, or fatty acids, are further classified as unsaturated or saturated, sometimes labeled good and bad fats respectively. Unsaturated fats have a double-bond structure and cannot only lower bad cholesterol (LDL) but also can also raise good cholesterol (HDL). These kinds of fats come from plant sources, such as olive oil and avocados.

Saturated fats, on the other hand, do not have this double bond and raise LDL levels, which can lead to atherosclerosis (plaque collecting in the arteries and narrowing them). Saturated fats come from animal sources, such as meat, milk, and eggs and fried foods.

Monounsaturated and Polyunsaturated Fatty Acids

Monounsaturated and polyunsaturated fatty acids are two different categories of unsaturated fats, one of two categories of fatty acids. (The other category is saturated fats.) These terms derive from the way the atoms are formed. If there is one double bond of carbon holding the fatty acid together, it is monounsaturated. If there are two or more double bonds of carbon holding the fatty acid together, it is polyunsaturated.

Monounsaturated fats are usually liquid when at room temperature. They include a host of natural oils: olive, grapeseed, flaxseed, and peanut, to name just a few. Monounsaturated fats lower so-called bad cholesterol (LDL).

Polyunsaturated fats come from a variety of sources, such as grains and oily fish. They provide benefits against cardiovascular disease and cancer.

Both fats provide needed elements that help the body run properly and are a necessary part of a balanced diet.

Purpose of Lipids

Although low-fat diets have been in vogue at various times, based on the misguided belief that fat is harmful, lipids serve a vital role in a healthy diet. Lipids have the most energy per gram when compared to other macronutrients, with nine calories per gram. Lipids are essential for carrying some vitamins, such as vitamin D, and are needed for calcium to be absorbed in the body.

Lipids are important for many other reasons:

- Body fat is used as a thermal layer and as an energy source for a nursing mother.
- Fats are needed for proper cell growth and regeneration.
- Fats digest more slowly and help a person feel full longer.
- Fat plays a role in endocrine function.

Digestion and Use of Lipids

Fat is digested along the entirety of the digestive tract. The process begins when it meets saliva. Body acids from the stomach and the intestines continue to break the fats down into components that can be used by the body. From the intestines, these components enter the bloodstream. The process goes like this:

- Lipids are broken down through the digestive tract
- Triglycerides are formed in the intestines
- Chylomicrons are formed in the lymphatic system
- Chylomicrons are distributed from the lymphatic system into the bloodstream

Triglycerides are broken down by the lipoprotein lipase (LPL) enzyme and used by body tissues, and the fat content can then be stored in muscle, organs, and fat cells.

Fat can be used as an immediate fuel source if the body has no available carbohydrate energy. However, if a person eats too much fat, it is far easier for the body to convert this into stored fat than it is for the body to alter excess carbohydrates chemically and store them as fat.

Satiety

Lipids have a very distinct effect on satiety, beginning with a hormonal response triggered in the mouth and stomach. Fats begin to trigger hormones that tell the brain the body is full. Fats also take longer to digest, giving the body a steady supply of fuel to process, leading to a full feeling for a longer period.

Many factors contribute to satiety beyond caloric intake (which is why people rarely feel full after drinking a high-calorie protein shake). Food volume and some of the actions of eating (such as crunching, ingesting mass, and getting a full stomach) are also important and cannot be satisfied by lipids alone.

A diet containing 30 percent fat or less will gain the benefits of containing fats while providing enough other foods and nutrients to satisfy a person's sensations of hunger.

INGESTING EXTRA FAT

There has been research in recent years regarding different types of lipids and how they might be used to the advantage of athletes and others who are engaged in fitness training. As a rule, fats take a long time to digest and are not necessarily the ideal supplement for sports or fitness activities.

However, some lipids can be more quickly digested for use in the body, namely medium-chain triglycerides. Unlike long-chain triglycerides, which are the most common types of lipids people ingest, medium-chain triglycerides do not go through such a long digestive process and can be used by the body more quickly.

While there is a theory that this energy could be a viable backup source for athletes, sparing glycogen sources, there is not enough current research to support this claim. Therefore, supplementation with fat should not be a top priority.

Metabolic syndrome is an umbrella term for a host of problems associated with digestive and endocrine problems such as diabetes, insulin resistance, obesity, and high blood pressure. People who tout protein-rich diets point to high carbohydrate consumption as being the underlying cause of metabolic syndrome, also known as syndrome X.

However, it seems more likely that the common denominator for these conditions is not carbohydrates, but rather an excess of free fatty acids. When free fatty acids are available, the body will use them first instead of more-optimal fuel sources, which in turn leads to problems processing glucose. This will lead to elevated insulin levels, which can then lead to insulin resistance and a host of other problems.

Therefore, it is more likely that higher fat content in the diet is the actual culprit, not high-carbohydrate diets.

CALORIC INTAKE

When a client's goal is to lose weight, the personal trainer needs to help the client assess their current caloric intake. Once daily caloric intake is documented, the trainer needs to help the client restrict empty or bad calories and also replace them where appropriate with good calories that will provide sufficient energy. Nutrient dense foods are high in nutrients and low in calories. Empty calorie foods are high in calories and low in nutrients. The client's calorie needs are based on activity level and weight loss goal. The client has nutritional needs that must be fulfilled within the caloric intake range. Eating nutrient dense foods makes it easier to meet nutritional needs within consuming additional calories. Empty calories make it challenging to meet nutritional need within the desired caloric range. Additionally, the trainer needs to help the client think of ways to increase her overall energy expenditure. When a client's goal is to gain weight, the process starts out the same way but differs in that the trainer will help her increase calorically dense foods and also increase her snacks throughout the day. Nutrient density and timing are important to provide sufficient energy for metabolic demands.

EDUCATING CLIENTS REGARDING ONGOING, SCIENTIFICALLY BASED INFORMATION

It is important for the personal trainer to educate clients in an ongoing fashion about proper exercise through scientific sources. The trainer must understand that clients will hear contradictory information on a daily basis regarding exercise and dietary techniques, and it is important to keep them abreast of information that is true and factual. Education can take place casually, and articles can be given to clients at regular intervals at the training session or can be emailed to them regularly.

Providing Opportunities for Community Involvement in Exercise

The personal trainer can provide opportunities for community involvement in exercise to help people participate. The trainer can help organize fun runs, provide group exercise sessions in the park, and organize classes to provide instruction on health and fitness. A community game day or field day can also be organized. The trainer can be active in writing for community blogs and internet sites to promote health and wellness.

Stress Management for Clients

The personal trainer can help the client identify stressful elements in their life and events that trigger stress. People feel stress from the pressures of daily life, or it can be a result of traumatic life events. The trainer should listen attentively to the client to identify stressors. It is appropriate to be supportive and offer basic stress management techniques such as breathing exercises and positive thinking. The trainer should stress that exercise is an excellent way to manage stress. The trainer should avoid attempting to solve the client's problem, and should refer the client to a psychologist if the client needs additional support. It is important for the client to have ownership in the problem-solving process, so they are invested in the positive outcome. The trainer can have a ready supply of professional staff to recommend to the client, for instance, licensed massage therapists, chiropractors, physical therapists, counselors, etc., to help in the process.

Legal, Professional, Business, and Marketing

Obtaining Medical Clearance

Stratifying Client Risk and Obtaining Medical Clearance to Minimize Negligence

Negligence is defined as the breach of the duty of care between a professional and a client. If a personal trainer doesn't take the time to stratify client risk and obtain medical clearance when appropriate, they are acting negligently and could be held liable if anything happens to the client during exercise programming. The personal trainer is obligated to do everything in their power to ensure the client is exercising in a safe environment with minimal risk to health and well-being; stratifying client risk and obtaining medical clearance meets this professional requirement.

Levels of Risk Stratification

The Health History Questionnaire enables clients to identify which risk factors affect them. For instance, the following risk factors could indicate coronary artery disease: hypertension, family history, high cholesterol, cigarette smoking, impaired fasting glucose, obesity, sedentary lifestyle. Additionally, the trainer needs to be aware of potential risk factors that may arise and periodically assess the client for signs of distress during the exercise session. The following risk factors could indicate pulmonary, metabolic, or cardiovascular disease:

- pain or tension in chest, neck, jaws, arms, or other areas
- dizziness
- shortness of breath
- orthopnea or nightly dyspnea
- palpitations
- ankle edema
- known heart murmur
- intermittent claudication
- unusual fatigue
- shortness of breath during normal activities

Clients can be stratified as low, moderate, or high risk based on the symptoms.

Risk Stratification

Risk Level	Applies to:	Criteria
Low risk	Asymptomatic men and women	Have ≤1 CVD risk factors
Moderate risk	Asymptomatic men and women	Have ≥2 CVD risk factors
High risk	Individuals with a known cardiovascular, pulmonary, or metabolic disease or that have any signs and symptoms those diseases.	

Medical Clearance Requirements

If a client answers yes to one or more questions indicating cardiovascular or metabolic or pulmonary disease and has a history of chronic disease, medical clearance is necessary to begin treatment through exercise. If a client answers yes to one or more of these questions, the personal trainer should take into account the health history as it is described by the client and should use his best judgment in recommending medical clearance or not. If the client was just barely placed in the moderate-risk category, but could be in the high-risk category very soon, medical clearance might be a good idea. Additionally, if the client responds poorly in the exercise testing, especially if she is unable to catch her breath or experiences heart palpitations, medical clearance is necessary.

Supervision for Individuals Who Received Medical Clearance

Clients who have received medical clearance for exercise should be monitored continually during the exercise session. The client should be familiar with the RPE scale and frequently communicate where they are on the scale throughout the workout session. These clients should never be left alone to exercise until they have come to a point where their risk factors are decreasing, or it is deemed that they can exercise safely by themselves.

Collaborating with Healthcare Professionals and Organizations

Continuing Education

A personal trainer should keep abreast of changes and modifications within the field through continuing education. Taking certification classes, subscribing to industry journals, and pursuing a degree in higher education are excellent ways to stay knowledgable and current. Training can be hands-on, online, or in a classroom setting. The important thing is for the trainer to consider how this education will increase their knowledge so that clients can ultimately benefit from it. The trainer should take classes that directly relate to the populations that they train.

Scope of Practice for Certified Personal Trainers

It is important for the personal trainer to know their scope of practice. Working within the scope of practice is important because it protects the trainer from liability issues and allows the trainer to focus on their area of expertise. Broadly, the scope of practice includes improving health and physical fitness as a means to prevent disease, health problems related to obesity, and premature aging. More specifically, personal trainers can help a client improve athletic performance, rehabilitate injuries, prevent injuries, and increase quality of life. Personal trainers should not diagnose injuries or medical problems and should not attempt to perform the role of a physical therapist, athletic trainer, registered dietitian, or rehabilitation specialist. Although the trainer may understand certain concepts from other allied fitness professional fields, he is not licensed to practice them.

If a personal trainer practices outside the acceptable scope of practice, it can lead to negligence and false practice of other professions. A client may become injured when a personal trainer attempts to teach things they are not licensed to practice. Doing this increases the personal trainer's liability, and ultimately the client could sue for any damages that are a result of false practice. A personal trainer could potentially lose their business in such a situation.

Effective Communication with Allied Professionals

If a client requires medical clearance to participate in a workout program, or has been referred to a personal trainer by a medical professional, it is appropriate to communicate regularly with a medical professional about the client's progress. Ideally, consultation takes place through phone calls or postal service. Sensitive information should never be left on an answering machine, to protect patient privacy. Furthermore, any sensitive information sent or received through email should be secured using private passwords and good email security standards, such as the use of encrypted email. The client also needs to be fully aware that information is being shared, and in the appropriate instances, sign a release of information.

Effective Relationships with Individuals in the Greater Health Community

The personal trainer should be aware that there are many different people invested in seeing a community grow in health and wellness. It is in the personal trainer's best interest to network with like-minded medical and allied health professionals in the community by attending professional events and creating a strong referral system for clients to seek additional help that is outside the personal trainer's scope of practice. The trainer can partner with other professionals to provide special package pricing that includes multiple sessions of personal training combined with other professional services. Being active in the community and attending community health events is the best way for personal trainers to network with other health practitioners to reach a common goal.

RECOMMENDING OTHER HEALTH SERVICES

When a personal trainer realizes that a client needs help in areas outside the trainer's scope of practice, the client needs to be referred. For instance, it is appropriate for the trainer to provide basic nutritional advice to the client, but the client should be referred to a registered dietician if the client wants a specific meal plan prescribed. It is important for the trainer to have a familiarity with the information on www.myplate.gov, such as the need to eat more vegetables, lean proteins, and natural foods, while avoiding processed foods and excessive red meat consumption as much as possible... If a client struggles excessively with finding solutions to stress management, and general guidelines for relaxation do not seem to suffice, the client should be referred to a life coach for further guidance.

Developing a Risk Management Program

CPR and AED

A personal trainer should maintain a current CPR/AED certification at all times. If a client becomes unconscious or stops breathing at any time, CPR protocol should be initiated. AED protocol should be initiated as necessary if there is more than one person at hand in a situation where a client collapses. It is important for the trainer to be familiar with the location of the AED in their club. If a personal trainer does not maintain a current CPR/AED certification, she could be held liable for practicing without a license.

Emergency Procedures Clearly Delineated for the Client

The personal trainer should discuss proper emergency procedure with the client. For instance, in case of a fire or inclement weather, the client should know where the exits are or where to seek adequate shelter. Whenever the fitness facility updates its procedures, it is the personal trainer's responsibility to ensure the client knows what to do. Additionally, the personal trainer should have on file permission from the client to call emergency services or a medical practitioner if appropriate.

Basic First-Aid Procedures

Exercise Intolerance

If a client is experiencing exercise intolerance, a cooldown should be initiated immediately to bring the client's heart rate back down to resting levels. The client needs to drink adequate amounts of water to maintain hydration. The client should continue moving as necessary until heart rate returns to normal. If the client feels dizzy or overheated, they can sit down, but lying down is contraindicated. The client should be given some cool water, and a cold towel or compress should be applied to the back of their neck to reduce body temperature. If the client is having trouble breathing due to chest pains, medical personnel should be contacted as it may be exercise-induced angina.

Exercise-Related Injury

If the client has an exercise-related injury, the client should be put in a sitting position and RICE (rest, ice, compression, elevation) should be followed for the injured area as needed (Note: This is untrue for a neck or spinal injury. A patient with a spinal injury should not be moved.). A medical practitioner should be immediately called. This information should be kept on file before any exercise sessions take place so it can be accessed in the event of an emergency. The personal trainer should also have on file a client's permission to call emergency services if it is deemed necessary in the event of an emergency.

Client Safety in the Fitness Facility

Client safety can be ensured by having them engage in exercises that correspond to their current fitness level. Clients should also be taught how to correctly handle resistance machines and free weights to avoid personal injury. They should be informed of facility rules regarding the flow of traffic inside the facility, appropriate cardiovascular machine usage, and age requirements for using the equipment. Clients should never use a machine they do not know how to use; this can be remedied by the personal trainer providing a comprehensive education on machine usage.

Injuries

A client may experience any of several common injuries, and it is beneficial for personal trainers to know how to work around them during an exercise session. Shin splints are characterized by pain along the outside of the leg starting right below the knee. A sprain is pain in the joint caused by an overstretched a ligament. A strain is characterized by muscle fibers tearing because of being overstretched. Bursitis is inflammation of the bursa sacs. Tendonitis is inflammation or irritation of a tendon. A fracture is a break in a bone. Patello-femoral pain syndrome is localized pain in front of the knee. Low back pain is localized pain across the lower back in the lumbar spine and pelvis. Plantar fasciitis is inflammation of the fascia on the bottom of the foot and often results in heel pain and tenderness.

Ailment	Symptoms
Shin splints	pain along the outside of the leg starting right below the knee
Sprain	pain in the joint caused by an overstretched a ligament
Strain	overstretched muscle fibers tearing
Bursitis	inflammation of the bursa sacs
Tendonitis	inflammation or irritation of a tendon
Fracture	break in a bone
Patellofemoral pain syndrome	localized pain in front of the knee
Low back pain	localized pain across the lower back in the lumbar spine and pelvis
Plantar fasciitis	inflammation of the fascia on the bottom of the foot

If shin splints, sprain, or strain occur during exercise, ice should be applied immediately and the ankle or other joint elevated. The client should be encouraged to wrap the area in a compression sleeve and visit a medical professional. If a fracture occurs, medical help should be sought immediately. A client with bursitis and tendonitis should engage in non–weight-bearing cardiovascular activities and resistance bands should be utilized during resistance activities. If a client has patello-femoral pain syndrome, medical clearance should be given before exercise, and non–weight-bearing cardiovascular activity should be the focus. Resistance activities should be focused around machine weights. For low back pain and plantar fasciitis, the warm-up and stretch segments should be extended, and myofascial release techniques should be utilized.

Contraindications to Exercises of the Major Muscle Groups

Even though some resistance exercises may be beneficial for many of the healthy population, they may be contraindicated in certain populations. When prescribing exercise, the trainer must account for physical limitations that prohibit the client from safely performing the exercise. During the exercise, the trainer must monitor the client for signs of distress or discomfort and adjust the program accordingly. For example, straight leg sit-ups and standing bent-over toe touches lose their exercise value for some people with neck and back issues because it places high compressional forces on the spinal column. Double leg raises can cause hyperextension of the lower back and place unnecessary stress on it, which is especially unneeded for clients who already have low back problems. Clients who are obese or have knee issues can cause undue stress by performing full squats. Overall, the personal trainer needs to assess potential exercise risk against reward when choosing exercises for the client.

Liability During Emergency Procedures

When an emergency situation happens, and the client is directly under the personal trainer's supervision, the personal trainer is held liable for what happens to the client. The personal trainer is responsible for the client's safety while performing exercise, and if an emergency occurs within the fitness facility, the trainer must do her best to ensure the client's safety. The trainer must be up-to-date on fitness and club emergency procedures.

Common Musculoskeletal Injuries

When a client is not fit, some common musculoskeletal injuries might take place. Although a trainer may do his best to monitor the client, there may be a pre-existing weakness that predisposes the client to injury. Some common injuries are as follows: contusion (bruising) of the muscle, sprain or strain of the muscle, fracture (including stress fractures with overuse or poor footwear) of the bones. The client must also be aware of any predispositions to injury and know what to do about an acute injury if she is exercising on her own. In addition, the program should be designed with this knowledge in mind.

Management and First-Aid During Exercise

Common Cardiovascular Complications

Cardiovascular events are rare in the healthy population. Pre-screening is important because it can identify individuals who may be at risk of an exercise induced cardiovascular event. If a cardiovascular event happens during an exercise session, the personal trainer needs to be aware of signs and symptoms that indicate it. The signs and symptoms are as follows: chest pain (or in head, neck, jaw, or arms), heart palpitations, hyperventilation, syncope, dyspnea, unusual shortness of breath during activities that typically do not bother the client, client's inability to speak. If any of these signs are present, the client may be suffering from exercise-induced angina, tachycardia, or asthma attack. If the symptoms do not go away when exercise activity ceases, medical personnel should be called immediately. If the symptoms do go away, the client needs to seek medical attention before resuming exercise at the next session.

Common Metabolic Abnormalities

If a client is experiencing a metabolic abnormality during exercise, such as hypo- (levels of < 80 mgldL) or hyperglycemia (fasting plasma glucose, > 126 mgldL), the trainer should be aware of signs that indicate it. Signs indicating metabolic abnormalities are as follows: fainting, syncope, pale face, blurred vision, dry mouth, excessive sweating. For clients with known metabolic abnormalities, it is recommended for them to bring something to eat or drink in case of emergency.

Open Wound

If a client arrives at a session with an open wound, the trainer should use discretion before continuing. If the wound appears treatable, the wound should be cleaned and bandaged before beginning the session. If the wound is more serious, the client should be referred to a physician and the session should be rescheduled. The safety of the client and other gym members is paramount. If a client has a wound that bleeds during an exercise session, the personal trainer should retrieve the first aid kit from the fitness facility. The client should be instructed to wash the wound with soap and water. The personal trainer should provide antiseptic and a band-aid, and if necessary, help apply dressing. If the trainer needs to apply dressing, she should wear safety gloves that are included in the first aid kit.

Complications with Musculoskeletal Injuries

If the pain does not interfere with the client's ability to express himself clearly, the personal trainer should ask the client what the pain feels like (i.e., sharp pain or dull pain); if the injury occurs in one of the limbs, the personal trainer needs to apply the RICE method where appropriate. If the injury is to the head, neck, or spine, the personal trainer needs to initiate emergency or first aid procedures depending on whether first aid staff are available at the fitness center. The trainer should never attempt to move the client in this situation. Additionally, to remain within the accepted scope of practice, the personal trainer should ask the client to seek medical attention to treat the injury.

Complications of Cardiovascular or Pulmonary Issues

If complications arise during an exercise session that could indicate cardiovascular or pulmonary issues, the trainer needs to instruct the client to lower the intensity of the exercise, assess heart rate to ensure it is coming down from where it was, and ask the client questions about how they feel to assess if they can talk. If the client can't talk, the intensity of the exercise needs to be lowered further. If heart rate remains erratic, or complications continue, the client needs to initiate cooldown. After cooldown, the trainer should stay with the client until heart rate is within 10 or fewer beats above the resting heart rate. Additionally, the client needs to drink water.

Complications Due to Metabolic Syndromes

If complications due to metabolic syndrome arise during an exercise session, the personal trainer needs to follow protocol similar to when complications are due to cardiovascular or pulmonary issues. The personal trainer must keep in mind that the client should never be left alone during this time. If reducing intensity of the workout helps the client reduce symptoms of complications, the trainer and client assess together that the client can continue the session, and no absolute contraindications are present, then the client can continue the session at the reduced intensity.

Ongoing Evaluation of Exercise Equipment

A fitness center should maintain its equipment according to manufacturer guidelines. Manufacturer handbooks should be kept on file and easily accessible. Machines should be cleaned between client use throughout the day, and clients should be encouraged and instructed on how to clean the machines as they finish with them. All equipment should be checked daily to ensure it is in proper working order.

Ensuring Safety Policies and Procedures Are Well-Known Among Clients

A fitness center should have all exits clearly marked. Procedures for emergency situations (fire, inclement weather, etc.) should be clearly posted. Additionally, the personal trainer should go through the procedures with clients to ensure understanding. Clients should be trained on equipment usage to avoid injury and to have confidence in using the fitness center on their own.

The personal trainer can assess client understanding of emergency procedures in a variety of ways. The trainer can verbally go through the steps of emergency response with the client. Additionally, he can practice the procedures with the client and allow time for questions regarding them. Ongoing assessment should occur. The trainer needs to be aware that it is his shared responsibility with the facility to ensure that the client understands all emergency procedures. The client should regularly practice all procedures.

If clients and staff do not properly understand how to act in an emergency situation, injuries can occur. Additionally, the fitness center can be held liable for any injuries or an unsafe situation that arises due to negligence. Procedures need to be put in place to safeguard the general well-being of the client/customer; if this is neglected, it becomes an issue of liability for the facility. If something were to happen to a client during an emergency that could have been avoided with proper training for the emergency situation, the fitness facility bears responsibility for that injury.

Necessary Steps of Emergency Action Plans

An emergency action plan for a fitness facility should consist of short, concise steps so clients and members can remember them. The emergency should be identified, a safe location should be designated in the proper area, and clients should be instructed on the proper path to that location. Emergency plans related to inclement weather (heavy thunderstorms or tornadoes) and fire should be in plain view and regularly practiced by facility staff and clients. Clients should be shown how to safely evacuate during a fire or seek appropriate shelter during a storm or tornado.

Spotting and Assisting During Exercise

Spotting and assisting clients with resistance activities allows the trainer to ensure they are using correct form and not lifting weight that is too heavy for them to be using. This is an active way to teach clients while allowing them to learn in an active way. Spotting and assisting ensure weights are not dropped, which prevents weights from rolling away and injuring others in the vicinity.

Continuing Education

Continuing education is essential for the personal trainer to stay informed on the latest research and techniques in the field. It also allows for trainers to get to know other professionals in the field. It keeps training techniques from becoming stagnant and ensures they are up-to-date and based on the most recent supporting research. Continuing education also allows personal trainers to specialize in a certain area and become aware of where their professional interests lie. Continuing education must come through approved providers to ensure that professionals are receiving the same level of education.

ACSM Requirements

For certified personal trainers, ACSM requires 45 hours of continuing education over every two-year period. Information for approved providers and courses can be found on ACSM's website (www.acsm.org)

Keeping Up-to-Date with Current Research

Current research allows personal trainers to maintain an understanding of changes in their field of practice and the scientific research that underlies those changes. This becomes important because trainers need to have a thorough understanding of their field and be aware of the most current information in an evolving field. Understanding this information allows them to synthesize it and explain it to their clients in a way that makes sense, which ultimately helps maintain motivation and adherence to their exercise program because they understand why they are performing the specified activities. In addition, up to date knowledge allows the trainer to design an effective program and meet the client's needs.

ACSM's Code of Ethics

The ACSM code of ethics is a set of standards that govern all ACSM licenses. It includes guidelines on ethical practice, disciplinary issues, and personal trainers' responsibility to the profession and to the public they serve. Some examples of ethics related to personal trainers are the following: they must respect their clients at all times, they may not take credit for the work of other professionals in their field, and they must not claim the ability to perform services for which they are not certified. Under the ACSM code of ethics, each ACSM member agrees to:

1. Abide by general ACSM principles
    a. Pursue continuous improvement and learning
    b. Uphold high standards
    c. Denounce unethical members
    d. Be concerned for the health and well-being of the community
2. Abide by specific ACSM principles
    a. Train athletes to play fairly
    b. Train athletes with care and professionalism
    c. Understand doping control standards
    d. Perform medical treatments only as qualified
    e. Refrain from aiding in doping
    f. Attempt to dissuade athletes from doping
    g. Protect confidentiality for clean athletes
    h. Understand and agree that unethical behavior can result in ACSM discipline
3. Remain in good-standing in regulated professions
4. Understand and abide by correct disclosure of affiliation
5. Approve and accept ACSM discipline

Review Video: Code of Ethics for Personal Trainers
Visit mometrix.com/academy and enter code: 810679

Professionalism in Dress and Behavior

It is important for the trainer to demonstrate professional conduct at all times. The trainer should always be respectful of all club patrons, employees, and their. Personal trainers show professionalism in the way they dress by wearing professional attire that is not too short or too tight. Collared shirts are preferred, as well as proper footwear. The personal trainer should also maintain a professional manner with the client and other colleagues. Eye contact should be used during conversations, along with a pleasant facial expression. Where appropriate, refer to men as "sir" and women as "ma'am" unless the client indicates otherwise. When introductions are made, clients should be referred to as "Mr.," "Mrs.," or "Ms." unless instructed otherwise.

Liability

Negligence

Personal trainers can be tempted to practice outside of the scope of their certification, especially when clients ask for their advice on topics better suited to a physical therapy or rehabilitation specialist. Clients frequently ask questions about diet that should be fielded by a licensed dietician. It is important for the trainer to focus on issues within their scope to avoid providing incorrect information. Staying in scope also reduces liability. It can also be tempting at the end of a long day for a personal trainer to become distracted and not pay attention to the client, which can increase the possibility of injury. Professionalism is of paramount importance. All clients should receive excellent service regardless of when the session occurs. In addition, when the trainer and client become very familiar with each other, they may be more likely to chat freely during the session. Conversation can cause the trainer to lose focus on the client's technique.

Risk Management Techniques to Minimize Liability

Personal trainers must take care to keep their eyes and ears open at all times for the safety of their clients. Cell phones and anything else that would be distracting to the trainer should be put away. Sessions should be properly documented, so if any questions arise, they can be answered in a timely way. Where necessary, the trainer should keep medical personnel up-to-date with pertinent information regarding the client. Clients should not be allowed to exercise on equipment that exceeds their current abilities, and trainers should not promise to help with training details that lie outside their scope of practice.

Equipment Maintenance and Client Safety

Equipment should be checked weekly to ensure it remains in proper working order. If it is not working properly, a sign should be put in clear view that puts the machine out of commission until maintenance can fix the issue. If equipment is broken, the client may be injured while trying to operate it.

Engaging in a Healthy Lifestyle

Modeling Positive Behaviors

One of the most important things the trainer can do for the client is to model positive behaviors. For instance, a courteous tone of voice when addressing the client, professional dress, actively listening to client issues, and not smoking are positive behaviors to demonstrate for the client. Additionally, it is best when the trainer models the behaviors that he expects from his clients; for instance, being early to appointments, eating with proper nutrition, and exercising consistently during the week. The trainer should have a "do as I do" attitude towards the client.

Manipulating Exercise Environment to Provide a Positive Experience

If the client is anxious about working out at a public fitness facility, the personal trainer can do a variety of things to ensure the client is comfortable. The trainer should start with machines that the client is a little more familiar and comfortable with before introducing foreign ones. The trainer should be early so she can greet the client, never making the client have to search for her to begin the session. If crowds make the client uncomfortable, the personal trainer can try to meet with the client during a time of day when the facility may be less crowded. The trainer should make sure the client knows where everything is located inside the facility and ensure he has all the tools he needs to be able to exercise alone.

Limiting Distractions During Training Sessions

Personal trainers can limit distractions during a training session simply by putting their phone away and not having conversations with others who happen to pass by. Additionally, trainers can limit conversation with clients during the session to what pertains to the exercise routine itself. Personal conversations can occur before or after the session. Clients should feel that all attention is on them for the duration of the session and that their money is going to a productive exercise session. Avoiding distractions makes the session safer and more enjoyable for the client.

Respecting Copyright

Safeguarding Personal Intellectual Property

The personal trainer may choose to copyright material that is his personal intellectual property. To accomplish this, the trainer needs to understand the basics of copyright laws and know where to find further information regarding the proper avenues for copyrighting material. Anything original to the personal trainer may be copyrighted and safeguarded in his name.

Documentation of Work Not Original to the Personal Trainer

Material that is not original to the personal trainer should be documented and cited whenever it is used. Trainers need to be aware that even though information may be well known publicly, it must still be cited when used on blogs, websites, or printed materials. At a minimum, the title of the resource, name of the author, when the resource was published, and where it can be found should be included in the citation.

Developing Original Educational Materials

It is for the personal trainer's benefit to have educational materials ready for clients before needing them. When a trainer first starts sessions with a client, she should ask the client what he would like to be educated on and perhaps allow them to choose from a variety of topics. Materials should be formatted so they are concise and easy to understand. All educational material should be properly cited unless the information is unique to the personal trainer. Having personal, original educational material is valuable for a trainer to have as part of her portfolio. Additionally, as the portfolio grows, it will benefit clients because they can choose from e a wide array of educational topics.

Protecting Client Confidentiality and Privacy Rights

Privacy and Confidentiality for Clients

The personal trainer can easily ensure privacy and confidentiality for a client by ensuring all computer files are password protected and information is shared only with those for whom the client has given permission. Information should optimally be shared over the phone or in person rather than email, or ideally, emails should be encrypted if they must be used. The rule of thumb is to make sure the client gives permission for passing on personal information.

Client privacy means that individual client information is privy only to the client it pertains to, and possibly to medical personnel. In some cases, the client may give permission for information to be shared with certain family members, but that permission should be obtained in writing from the client. Personal client information should never be shared over social media or with other trainers.

FERPA and HIPAA Laws

The FERPA (Family Educational Rights and Privacy Act) and HIPAA (Health Insurance Portability and Accountability Act) laws protect the privacy of the individual. In personal training, the trainer should only share what is minimally necessary for the benefit of the client and only where permission has been obtained. Client information should also be stored in a safe place that doesn't have public access, preferably under lock and key.

The personal trainer should follow FERPA and HIPAA guidelines when appropriate for his practice. Since health information is private and confidential, the trainer needs to take every precaution to ensure it is not accidentally shared with inappropriate outside sources. The trainer needs to make a practice of filing and locking client information and keeping it in his office rather than taking it to his place of residence.

Client Health and Contact Information

Before a training session, the personal trainer should always have the client's file where emergency contact information can be easily found. The trainer should never begin a training session without having that client's file. The file can include session notes and previous workout sessions. This way, if the client has questions about her progress, the information is easily accessible in the moment.

ACSM Practice Test

1. What are the primary, functional movements?

a. Bend-and-lift, single-leg, pushing, pulling, and rotational
b. Bend-and-lift, single-leg, jumping, and pushing/pulling
c. Single-leg, jumping, pushing, and pulling
d. Jumping, pushing, rotational, and multidirectional

2. The American Heart Association (AHA) dictates there will be what maximum interval between trainings to maintain a cardiopulmonary resuscitation (CPR) qualification?

a. 12 months
b. 3–12months
c. 24 months
d. 36 months

3. Which of the following choices is an example of a synovial bicondylar joint?

a. Elbow
b. Ankle
c. Knee
d. Hip

4. Flexion and extension of the glenohumeral joint cause movement in what plane of motion?

a. Sagittal
b. Frontal
c. Axial
d. Transverse

5. Which key movement would best help a client improve his or her functional rotational movement?

a. Unilateral rows
b. Hay balers
c. Thoracic matrix
d. Bilateral presses

6. What percentage of total calorie consumption should be from fat?

a. 10–35 percent
b. 20–35 percent
c. 10–25 percent
d. 20–30 percent

7. Which of the following is NOT required as a minimum to reduce additional risks in a fitness facility setting?

a. Clean water or drinking supply
b. Adequate lighting
c. Staffing and supervision
d. Member training for use of equipment

8. What muscles of the scapulothoracic joint are the major agonists when performing a push-up?

a. Serratus anterior, pectoralis minor, trapezius, levator scapulae, and rhomboids
b. Anterior deltoid, pectoralis minor, supraspinatus, and rhomboids
c. Serratus anterior, pectoralis major, biceps, and triceps
d. Anterior deltoid, biceps, levator scapulae, and trapezius

9. During a 6-month review with your client, he has decided that his current gains in strength are substantial enough that he would like to move to a maintenance program. What term best describes the close of this portion of his program?

a. Variable goals
b. End review
c. Capping
d. Evaluation

10. What is considered a normal level for triglycerides?

a. <150
b. <500
c. 150–199
d. 200–499

11. All of the following are reasons that a personal trainer should never recommend supplements to a client EXCEPT

a. that supplement manufacturing companies usually do not carry insurance, leaving the personal trainer 100 percent liable for monetary compensation should either be sued.
b. that supplements are not regulated by the Food and Drug Administration (FDA).
c. that underlying and/or unknown medical conditions may be exacerbated by supplement use.
d. that a trainer should always review a client's 3-day food log before recommending nutrient supplementation.

12. As a client's abilities increase and his or her body adapts to the stimulus of training, it will be necessary to increase the intensity of the stimulus to continue to see increased results. What is this principle known as?

a. Progressive overload
b. Prioritization of training
c. Variation in training
d. Overload

13. What would be the ideal performance test for a first-time client, new to fitness, who would like help returning to fitness after leading a sedentary lifestyle for the past three years?

a. 1.5-Mile Test
b. Rockport 1-Mile Test
c. Queens College Step Test
d. Astrand-Rhyming Test

14. It is recommended that a personal trainer hold a minimum of what amount of professional liability insurance?

a. $1 million
b. $2 million
c. $200,000
d. $150,000

15. Which of the following is likely NOT a factor that plays into behavior change?

a. Readiness for change
b. Perceived self-efficacy
c. Scheduling
d. Cost

16. What level of nutrition guidance is within the scope of practice for a personal trainer?

a. Share public information, and help interpret public information such as that found in the US Department of Agriculture (USDA) Food Guide Pyramid and the dietary guidelines of the Academy of Nutrition and Dietetics.
b. Write a meal plan using the public information such as that found in the USDA Food Guide Pyramid and the dietary guidelines of the Academy of Nutrition and Dietetics.
c. Write a meal plan such as that found in the USDA Food Guide Pyramid and the dietary guidelines of the Academy of Nutrition and Dietetics, and provide or recommend supplements to fill in nutritional inadequacies due to the lifestyle of the client.
d. Recommend certain eating trends such as veganism, ketogenic, or Paleo, according to the needs and goals of the client, using public information found in the USDA Food Guide Pyramid and the dietary guidelines of the Academy of Nutrition and Dietetics.

17. The most important predictors for behavior change, according to Social Cognitive Theory, are the expectations of results and what other principle?

a. Motivation
b. Self-efficacy
c. Goal setting
d. Extrinsic motivation

18. You have a client who is male, 47 years old, who is looking to increase his range of motion (ROM) and decrease tightness in his joints. What is the most beneficial flexibility programming for this client?

a. At least 5 minutes after each training session
b. At least 10 minutes for a minimum of 1 day per week
c. At least 10 minutes daily
d. At least 5 minutes for a minimum of 3 days per week

19. How many vertebrae make up the lumbar curve of the spine?

a. 8
b. 5
c. 12
d. 7

20. You meet a client who has been exercising on her own for the past 3 months. She has a plan of action and a steady routine at the local gym. Which stage of change is this client in, per the Transtheoretical Model?

a. Contemplation
b. Preparation
c. Action
d. Maintenance

21. What is the maximum daily caloric deficit recommended for weight loss?

a. 400 kcals
b. 500 kcals
c. 1,000 kcals
d. 2,000 kcals

22. What is the baseline recommendation for cardiorespiratory programming of moderate intensity?

a. At least 30 minutes per day on at least 5 days per week
b. At least 15 minutes per day on at least 5 days per week
c. At least 45 minutes per day on at least 3 days per week
d. At least some moderate activity at least 4 days per week

23. What key coping strategy is most important for relapse prevention?

a. Social support
b. Assertiveness
c. Self-regulation
d. Intrinsic motivation

24. During an initial conversation with a new client, he states that he made the appointment with you at the behest of a family member and that he doesn't care about his own unhealthy behaviors. By the end of the conversation, he has shifted his attitude and is eager to begin working with you. What technique did you most likely use to inspire this change?

a. Empathy
b. Motivational interviewing
c. Active listening
d. Building rapport

25. Which communication form requires trust, attention, and understanding to be effective?

a. Rapport
b. Active listening
c. Periphrasis
d. Facial expressions

26. According to the criteria set by American College of Sports Medicine (ACSM), all of the following are positive risk factors on a Medical Health Screening EXCEPT

a. myocardial infarction before the age of 55 in father or male first-degree relative.
b. body mass index ≥ to 30 kg/m2.
c. systolic blood pressure ≥ 135 mmHg.
d. impaired fasting glucose (IFG).

27. What is the only negative risk factor in the American College of Sports Medicine (ACSM) risk stratification criteria?

a. High-serum HDL cholesterol ≥ 60 mg/dl (1.55mmol/L)
b. Total serum cholesterol ≥ 200 mg/dl (5.18 mmol/L)
c. Prescribed antihypertensive medication
d. Quit smoking cigarettes within the past 6 months

28. All the following are characteristics of a SMART goal EXCEPT

a. specific.
b. measurable.
c. affordable.
d. time-bound.

29. You are working with a new client, and you have asked her to write down her weight loss goals using the SMART guidelines. Which is an example of a SMART goal?

a. To lose 20 lbs, in the next 30 days by increasing participation in cardio exercise and playing sports with friends
b. To lose 10 lbs, over the next 2 months by performing 30 minutes of cardiovascular activity three times a week and weight training one time a week so that she can prepare to try out for the local soccer team
c. To lose 10 lbs, so that the client may purchase the new swimsuit
d. To lose weight by increasing cardiovascular activity to three times week and lifting weights two times a week

30. A potential client is referred to you by a doctor and calls to schedule the initial consultation. During your meeting, he informs you that he does not want to schedule the first session just yet, and he is merely gathering information. Per the Transtheoretical Model of behavior change, this client is at which stage of change?

a. Precontemplation
b. Contemplation
c. Preparation
d. Action

31. Which model of behavior change is dependent on the weighing of barriers to change and the perceived benefits of change?

a. Transtheoretical Model
b. Theory of Planned Behavior
c. The Health Belief Model
d. Social Cognitive Theory

32. The most successful goals are those that are all of the following EXCEPT

a. client selected.
b. SMART.
c. self-monitored.
d. flexible.

33. The anatomical position can be described as which of the following?

a. The body is erect, feet together, arms at the sides with palms facing forward, thumbs pointed away from the body, and fingers extended.
b. The body is erect, feet hip width apart, arms at the sides with palms facing forward, thumbs pointed away from the body, and fingers extended.
c. The body is erect, feet together, arms at the sides with palms facing forward, thumbs pointed away from the body, and fingers flexed.
d. The body is erect, feet hip width apart, arms at the sides with palms facing rear, thumbs pointed toward the body, and fingers extended.

34. What type of joint is the glenohumeral?

a. Ball-and-socket
b. Ellipsoidal
c. Bicondylar
d. Hinge

35. A person performing an adduction of the hip joint and engaging the adductor longus, brevis, and magus, gracilis, and pectineus is likely performing which exercise?

a. Leg raise
b. Machine hip abduction
c. Broomstick twist
d. Lunge

36. The scapulothoracic joint is formed by the articulation of the thoracic cage and scapula. In the kinetic chain, movement of this joint results in movement of these other joints EXCEPT

a. acromioclavicular.
b. glenoid fossa.
c. glenohumeral.
d. sternoclavicular.

37. Which postural deviation will increase lordosis in the lumbar spine?

a. Anterior pelvic tilt
b. Adduction of the scapulae
c. Scapular winging
d. Posterior pelvic tilt

38. While walking the gym floor, a potential client approaches you asking for advice with increasing muscle strength and size. This client is looking for information regarding which adaptation?

a. Atrophy
b. Hypertrophy
c. Endurance
d. Hyperplasia

39. During the initial assessment phase of the client-trainer relationship, which assessment would logically be administered after both the resting heart rate and resting blood pressure measurements have been established?

a. Flexibility
b. Body composition
c. Cardiovascular assessment
d. Muscular fitness

40. After conducting body composition assessments on four clients, which produced measurements in the normal range?

a. A female with a body mass index (BMI) of 25.1
b. A male with a BMI of 18.3
c. A male with a BMI of 21.2
d. A female with a BMI of 32

41. During the initial consultation with a new client, you learn that she is being treated for stable coronary artery disease (CAD). She has no ongoing issues and has been stable for more than six months. What is the best course of action for this client?

a. Begin regular programming with the client.
b. Schedule a second session with the client and ask that she speak with her physician between now and then.
c. Require the client complete Release of Liability and Informed Consent forms.
d. Obtain a physician's medical clearance.

42. Which of the following is a physiological benefit of beginning an exercise program?

a. Improvement in bone health
b. Enhanced feeling of well-being
c. Better cognitive function
d. Decreased anxiety and depression

43. A decreased risk of falls and what other benefit of exercise are specific to older adults?

a. Increased metabolic rate
b. Positive effect on stress
c. Improved cognitive function
d. Weight loss and reduced obesity

44. Each of the following is a major sign or symptom suggestive of pulmonary, metabolic, or cardiovascular disease EXCEPT

a. syncope.
b. fatigue.
c. ankle edema.
d. orthopnea.

45. During the initial consultation with a new client, he states his current activity consists of training with resistance bands at home to a workout DVD and an occasional run in the evenings when he has time after work. What is this client's aerobic activity status and the associated training focus?

a. Beginner: no prior activity
b. Beginner: minimal activity
c. Intermediate: minimal activity
d. Intermediate: fair to average fitness

46. Flexibility and resistance training for pregnant women in which position should be avoided after what point in pregnancy?

a. Supine; after the second trimester
b. Prone; after 6 weeks
c. Supine; after the first trimester
d. Prone; as soon as the client knows she is pregnant

47. Each of these are a special precaution a personal trainer should take when working with a client with diabetes EXCEPT

a. keeping a vigilant eye out for the warning signs or hypo- and hyperglycemia.
b. having the client eat 1 to 2 hours prior to exercise.
c. having fruit juice available.
d. having the client eat a snack if blood glucose reads more than 100mg/dl.

48. What types of training are the most effective way to improve an athlete's stride rate and frequency?

a. Sprint, plyometric, strength, and ballistic training
b. Cardiovascular, plyometric, and ballistic training
c. Resistance, ballistic, cardiovascular, and plyometric training
d. Sprint, plyometric, and strength training

49. A person who is exercising at a moderate to high altitude must reduce the intensity of a workout to keep the heartrate in its target zone. This is a result of what characteristic of blood at a high altitude?

a. Density
b. Oxygenation
c. Pressure
d. Temperature

50. Which resistance training progression technique utilizes the micro-cycle as the timing basis for intervals and intensity?

a. Reverse linear programming
b. Nonlinear periodized programs
c. Linear periodization programming
d. Progressive overload

51. Which is the only type of stretching that does NOT need to follow the warm-up component of an exercise program?

a. Dynamic stretching
b. Proprioceptive neuromuscular facilitation (PNF)
c. Static stretching
d. Passive stretching

52. What is the appropriate length of time for the cool-down phase of a training session?

a. 2–4 minutes
b. 5–10 minutes
c. 10–15 minutes
d. 3–5 minutes

53. A client who suffers from a hernia may be further injured by any activity that increases pressure in the abdominal cavity. Which breathing technique should never be used with one of these clients?

a. Timed breathing
b. Pranayama
c. Valsalva maneuver
d. Yogic

54. In terms of reversibility of resistance training, what is the rate at which an individual will lose his or her strength if the client completely stops resistance training at any point?

a. One-third the rate it was gained
b. One-half the rate it was gained
c. One-fourth the rate it was gained
d. One-third total mass in the same time it was gained

55. Which is true of proper spotting technique during resistance training?

a. Keep hands as far from the weights as possible as to not obstruct the movement.
b. Remove the weight collars and clips when a client is exceeding his or her personal maximum.
c. Allow the client to count his or her own repetitions and signal to you when he or she is finished.
d. Assist any time the predetermined speed decreases.

56. A client who is incorrectly performing a resistance training movement would likely benefit most from which cues to correct form?

a. Imagery, affirmational, and visual
b. Alignment, safety, and tactile
c. Visual, wrong/right, and tactile
d. Breathing, visual, and motivational

57. Which is NOT a characteristic of proper weight lifting technique?

a. Use the correct grip.
b. Keep the abdominals tight.
c. Use distinct, segmented motions.
d. Keep the weight close.

58. During the initial consultation with a new client, she informs you that her main goal will be training for a marathon. As a fitness professional, you design a program that progresses in stages that mimic the physical demands of a marathon. The specific exercises you chose to train her with will stimulate the adaptations she will need to complete a marathon. Which principle of specificity should you use to design this client's program?

a. Prioritization
b. Specific Adaptations to Imposed Demands (SAID)
c. Resistance training
d. Cardiovascular prioritization

59. During an evaluation of the lower body's kinetic chain, you notice an abduction of the client's knees between the femur and tibia, and the ankles are collapsed medially. This client has which postural deviation?

a. Pronation with external rotation of the knee
b. Supination with internal rotation of the knee
c. Neutral subtalar position
d. Pronation with internal rotation of the knee

60. Which of the following is the only form to identify coronary heart disease (CHD) risk factors in potential clients?

a. Medical history
b. Physical Activity Readiness Questionnaire (PARQ)
c. Informed consent
d. Physician's clearance

61. What is the average amount of hip flexion required to perform a correct squatting motion?

a. 95 percent
b. 135 percent
c. 95 degrees
d. 135 degrees

62. What is the purpose of the hip hinge motion when teaching the correct way to perform a squat?

a. To promote quad dominance over glute dominance
b. To promote glute dominance over quad dominance
c. To promote hip alignment over the knees and feet
d. To promote alignment between the trunk and tibia

63. Which activities would you recommend for training children with the goal of bone strengthening?

a. Hopscotch, skipping, and jumping
b. Tug-of-war and tree climbing
c. Walking and bicycle riding
d. Swimming, skiing, and running

64. What is the proper progression when teaching and performing bilateral and unilateral chest presses?

a. Standing press, single-arm press with contralateral stance, and single-arm press with ipsilateral stance
b. Seated press, standing press, single-arm press with contralateral stance, and single-arm press with ipsilateral stance
c. Seated press, seated single-arm press, seated double-arm press, and standing press with wide leg stance
d. Seated press, standing press with staggered leg stance, and standing press with wide leg stance

65. What is the proper progression of the wood chop, rotational movement, exercise?

a. Long moment arm, standing short moment arm, standing long moment arm, hip hinge/squat, long moment arm, and full chop
b. Standing long moment arm, hip hinge/squat, and full chop
c. Long moment arm, short moment arm, hip hinge/squat, and full chop
d. Long moment arm, standing long moment arm, hip hinge/squat, and full chop

66. After a particularly difficult exercise, you look your client in the eye, acknowledge the effort he put in to the work, and compliment his form. What training tactic are you communicating?

a. Stimulus control
b. Positive reinforcement
c. Shaping
d. Behavior chains

67. Which of the following would be the most effective way to teach a client a new movement?

a. Identify the movement, detail the exercise, demonstrate the movement, and have the client attempt the exercise.
b. Demonstrate the movement, have the client begin the movement, and detail the exercise while cueing client corrections.
c. Identify the movement, demonstrate the movement, detail the exercise, and demonstrate the movement again.
d. Demonstrate the movement, identify the movement, detail the movement, and demonstrate the movement again.

68. The exercise continuum is a scale from left (1) to right (6) that is used to rate the difficulty of an exercise. Which way would the trainer be moving an exercise if he or she must modify it for an unconditioned client?

a. Left
b. Right
c. Up
d. Down

69. You have completed the initial consultation with a new client. Given the information provided, you have set appropriate goals and designed a 12-week program. You prepared your client for a certain level of self-monitoring and prepped a schedule for the upcoming weeks. What important part of physical activity behavior change is missing?

a. Positive reinforcement
b. Feedback
c. Intervention
d. Customization

70. Which model of behavior change states that self-efficacy and expectations are the most important factors for behavior change?

a. Health Belief Model
b. Goal Setting Theory
c. Social Cognitive Theory
d. Theory of Planned Behavior

71. A client who has dyslipidemia has what?

a. Lowered HDL
b. Elevated LDL
c. Elevated LDL and total cholesterol
d. Elevated total cholesterol

72. A client's food log reveals she ate 40 grams of carbohydrates, 16 grams of protein, and 9 grams of fat for lunch yesterday. How many calories did your client consume during that meal?

a. 260 calories
b. 305 calories
c. 385 calories
d. 297 calories

73. You notice your client has recorded weight fluctuations of more than 10 pounds over the past few self-monitored weigh-ins. He claims to still be feeling fat, despite having lost 15 percent of his original body weight since starting your program, and his food log shows minimal entries. Despite having made great progress so far, and being only halfway to his weight goal, your client is continually stopping to look in the mirror during sessions and appears uncomfortable. What is most likely going on with your client?

a. This client may be suffering from a loss of motivation and would benefit from a change in programming.
b. This client may be suffering from sickness and not feeling well.
c. This client may be suffering from an eating disorder.
d. This client may be entering the maintenance stage, and programming should shift from a weight loss goal to a resistance training/strength training-focused program.

74. What is the recommendation for water consumption for exercisers?

a. Drink approximately 800 mL of fluid about 2 hours before exercise
b. Drink approximately 800 mL of fluid about 90 minutes before exercise
c. Drink approximately 500 mL of fluid about 90 minutes before exercise
d. Drink approximately 500 mL of fluid about 2 hours before exercise

75. Your 16-year-old female client is experiencing energy imbalances, menstrual disturbances, and a decrease bone mineral density. What disorder is she likely suffering from?

a. Anorexia nervosa
b. Bulimia nervosa
c. Female Athlete Triad
d. Binge-eating disorder

76. How many kcals are in 1 gram of carbohydrates?

a. 9
b. 7
c. 5
d. 4

77. Which is NOT true of relapse?

a. It is an inevitable part of the work of a personal trainer.
b. Talking to clients about relapse before it occurs may prevent it.
c. Regulating the schedule of a client with poor time-management skills can help prevent relapse.
d. A personal trainer should prepare a client for relapse from Day 1 of the training program.

78. Clients wishing to increase muscle mass should perform muscle-building exercises and consume how many more calories per day?

a. This depends on the client
b. None
c. 250–350 kcals
d. 500–700 kcals

79. Which is NOT a result of eating smaller, more frequent meals?

a. Lower body fat
b. Increase of metabolic rate
c. Maintenance of muscle mass
d. Lower stress hormone levels

80. A client weighs 210 lbs. and has a body fat percentage of 21 percent. What is the weight of his or her lean body mass?

a. 166 lbs.
b. 44 lbs.
c. 189 lbs.
d. 171 lbs.

81. Under which theories of law would a personal trainer be liable to training a client in an unsafe environment?

a. Malpractice
b. Tort
c. Negligence
d. Liability

82. A first aid kit containing a cardiopulmonary resuscitation (CPR) micro-shield is stocked for what emergency procedure?

a. Mouth-to-mouth resuscitation
b. Mouth-to-mask ventilations
c. Automated external defibrillation
d. Mask-to-mouth defibrillation

83. What is another name for the whole-part-whole teaching method?

a. Demo-detail-demo
b. Tell, show, do
c. Demo-show-demo
d. Tell, show, cue

84. While training a client on the facility's main floor, you observe another member trying to operate a machine, but the machine is malfunctioning. What should you do?

a. Excuse yourself from your client, and remove the machine or have it removed, from the gym floor until it can be repaired.
b. Place an "out of order" sign on the machine.
c. Do not leave your client. After the session, take steps to have the machine repaired and/or replaced.
d. Apologize to the member, and unplug the machine to prevent further inconveniences.

85. A regular member of your gym approaches you asking for advice for pain that is running along the outside of his thigh to his knee, and you recommend myofascial release. What overuse injury is he likely suffering from?

a. Lateral epicondylitis
b. Tendinitis
c. Iliotibial band syndrome (ITBS)
d. Bursitis

86. Which injury is defined as a stop in continuation of bone continuity?

a. Sprain
b. Strain
c. Hypoxia
d. Fracture

87. The exercise continuum is a scale from left (1) to right (6) that is used to rate the difficulty of an exercise. When giving your client an exercise to perform, you notice she moves the weight with ease. You decide to move the exercise from a 4 to a 5 on the exercise continuum. What is this called?

a. Modification
b. Engagement
c. Progression
d. Conditioning

88. Which of the following is NOT a major type of hypoperfusion?

a. Obstructive
b. Hypovolemic
c. Destructive
d. Cardiogenic

89. Which grade of musculoskeletal strain identifies many muscle fibers that are injured, severe tenderness, and muscle pain with mild swelling, possible bruising, and a noticeable loss of function?

a. I
b. II
c. III
d. IV

90. Which part of the knee performs the functions of joint congruency, lubrication, stability, shock absorption, and proprioception?

a. Menisci
b. Anterior cruciate ligament (ACL)
c. Medial collateral ligament (MCL)
d. Patella cartilage

91. Which type of business arrangement is popular among personal trainers, allows the trainer to work on her own, charge her own fees, and create her own schedule while being temporarily employed at a large fitness facility?

a. Partnership
b. Independent contractor
c. Sole proprietor
d. Salaried employee

92. Which of the following is NOT an element a plaintiff must establish in court to substantiate a charge of negligence?

a. The trainer had a duty to protect the plaintiff from injury.
b. Damage occurred.
c. Damage was directly caused by the trainer.
d. The damage was caused by proximate causation.

93. Which is the federal law that protects the privacy of student education records?

a. USDHHS
b. FERPA
c. HIPAA
d. USDoE

94. What is the process of weighing the pros and cons of behavior change with a client during intervention called?

a. Decisional balance
b. Transtheoretical modeling (TTM)
c. Cognitive strategies
d. Behavioral strategies

95. Professional liability insurance typically covers a broad spectrum of claims EXCEPT

a. sexual harassment.
b. negligence.
c. breach of contract.
d. short-term disability.

96. When training a client in his or her home, you can have the client provide his or her own music selection. This helps to avoid which incidence?

a. Trademark infringement
b. Royalty fees
c. Copyright infringement
d. Offending the client

97. As a personal trainer, you want to start training clients in your own home. You should take which precaution to ensure your financial protection?

a. Incorporate your business
b. Add an insurance rider to your policy
c. Advertise your business only within permitted limits
d. Use a separate, business entrance to adhere to housing standards

98. Effective programming will be different for each client based on his or her fitness level and goals. However, program progression follows what important rule for all clients?

a. Increase repetitions for faster improvements in strength and technique.
b. Single sets are more beneficial than super sets.
c. Increase weight loads for faster improvements in strength and technique.
d. Always begin with a light weight when teaching a new skill.

99. Which functional exercise improves thoracic extension?

a. Supine 90-90
b. Rocking quadrupeds
c. Shoulder bridge
d. Spinal extensions and spinal twists

100. How many positive risk factors must a client have to be considered a moderate risk?

a. 0
b. 1
c. 2
d. Any known cardiovascular, pulmonary, or metabolic disease

101. Each of these is a physiological adaptation to aerobic conditioning at submaximal effort EXCEPT

a. decrease in resting heart rate.
b. decrease in cardiac output.
c. increase in stroke volume.
d. increase in maximum minute ventilation.

102. In reference to behavioral strategies, which of the following is the process of gradually achieving a desired behavior by using reinforcements?

a. Observational learning
b. Shaping
c. Stimulus control
d. Extinction

103. In what year did the Health Insurance Portability and Accountability Act (HIPAA) become a federal law?

a. 1996
b. 1989
c. 1992
d. 1986

104. A client is showing signs of overuse from additional training she has been performing separate from personal training sessions. She complains of pain in the anterior lower leg. She is most likely suffering from which injury?

a. Iliotibial band syndrome (ITBS)
b. Shin splints
c. Bursitis
d. Lateral epicondylitis

105. Each of the following are signs of overtraining and should signal to the trainer to decrease intensity and/or frequency of training EXCEPT

a. decreased resting hear rate.
b. increased resting heart rate.
c. disturbed sleep.
d. decreased hunger.

106. Under which business structure is the owner or owners protected from liability through the creation of a separate entity?

a. Partnerships
b. Sole proprietorship
c. Limited liability company (LLC)
d. Express partnership

107. Which is NOT a characterization of binge-eating disorder?

a. Rapid eating
b. Purging
c. Eating alone
d. Eating when not hungry

108. Personal trainers who are involved in partnerships or corporations should consider purchasing which insurance in addition to their professional liability policy?

a. Keyman insurance
b. Umbrella insurance
c. Product liability insurance
d. Disability insurance

109. You client approaches you three days after your second session together and complains of swelling, pain, and extreme soreness in the muscles targeted in the session. What injury is this client most likely suffering from?

a. Muscle strain
b. Exhaustion
c. Delayed onset muscle soreness (DOMS)
d. Muscle sprain

110. What is the lean mass percentage of a client with a body fat percentage of 17 percent?

a. 83 percent
b. 17 percent
c. 5.88 percent
d. 1.2 percent

111. The primary role of which ligament is to prevent medial valgus on the knee?

a. Medial collateral ligament (MCL)
b. Anterior cruciate ligament (ACL)
c. Posterior cruciate ligament (PCL)
d. Meniscus

112. What is the name of the plane of motion that divides the body into right and left sides?

a. Frontal
b. Sagittal
c. Axial
d. Transverse

113. Which of the following is NOT one of the four elements of active listening?

a. Listening to spoken statements
b. Identifying statements that indicate learning opportunities
c. Observing nonverbal cues
d. Exhibiting understanding through the use of local expressions and industry terminology

114. What is the term used to describe the ratio of lean body mass to body fat?

a. Body composition
b. Body fat percentage
c. Body mass index (BMI)
d. Body fat distribution

115. As a personal trainer, obtaining your cardiopulmonary resuscitation (CPR), automated external defibrillator (AED), and first aid training, creating an emergency response plan, and having written emergency procedures are all part of what part of business?

a. Risk management
b. Initial public offering (IPO)
c. Accountability structure
d. Audits

116. What kind of learner is the majority of the population?

a. Kinesthetic
b. Auditory
c. A combination of visual, auditory, kinesthetic
d. Visual

117. Which form is considered an agreement between the client and personal trainer and works in conjunction with the informed consent?

a. Physical Activity Readiness Questionnaire (PARQ)
b. Medical history form
c. Self-assessment
d. Release of liability

118. Stress management is an important part of any good program. As a trainer, you should encourage clients to participate in stress-reducing activities such as massage therapy or guided imagery, which decreases catecholamine and cortisol production from which gland?

a. Apocrine
b. Eccrine
c. Sebaceous
d. Adrenal

119. What percentage of body fat is required by men and women for thermoregulation, hormone production, insulation, maintenance of certain body functions, and maintenance of overall health?

a. Between 2 and 5 percent for men and between 5 and 15 percent for women
b. Between 2 and 5 percent for men and between 10 and 13 percent for women
c. Between 4 and 7 percent for men and between 10 and 13 percent for women
d. Between 4 and 10 percent for men and between 5 and 13 percent for women

120. Which is true of a client who has been determined to have moderate risk during risk classification?

a. Doctor supervision during submaximal testing is required.
b. The client has one risk factor.
c. The client requires a medical exam prior to moderate exercise.
d. A medical exam is required before vigorous exercise.

121. A client consumes the following: 10 grams of carbohydrate, 4 grams of protein, 2 grams of fiber, and 5 grams of fat. Which macronutrient contributed most significantly to the client's total calorie intake?

a. Fiber
b. Protein
c. Carbohydrate
d. Fat

Answer Key and Explanations

1. A: The five primary functional movements are bend-and-life, single-leg, pushing, pulling, and rotational. These should be taught and evaluated prior to teaching clients any movement patterns or progressing to weight-bearing exercises.

2. C: Although the AHA recommends training refreshers every 3 to 12 months after initial CPR qualification, they state that there will be a maximum of 2 years between training sessions to maintain the certification; after the 2-year mark, the qualification will no longer be valid.

3. C: The knee is an example of a bicondylar joint. The elbow is a hinge joint. The talocrural ankle joint is a hinge, and the subtalar ankle is a gliding joint. The hip is a ball-and-socket joint.

4. A: Flexion and extension of the glenohumeral joint cause movement in the sagittal plane. Abduction and adduction of this joint cause movement in the frontal plane, and internal and external rotation of the glenohumeral joint cause movement in the transverse (axial) plane.

5. B: Hay balers require stabilization of the core in all three planes of motion, and the weight transference through the hips and legs help gain leverage and maintain balance. Unilateral rows perform the pull motion, and bilateral presses perform the push motion. A thoracic matrix also performs a push motion but through the entire kinetic chain.

6. B: It is recommended that 20 to 35 percent of total calorie consumption should be from fats; 45 to 65 percent of total calories should be carbohydrates; and 10 to 35 percent should be protein.

7. D: Clean drinking water, adequate lighting, adequate staffing and supervision, and nonslip surfaces are among the many steps a facility must take to minimize risk. Caution signs must be posted near machines, but the facility does not need to provide training to each new member. Many facilities offer new member orientation classes, but these are considered far above the minimum requirements.

8. A: The serratus anterior, pectoralis minor, trapezius, levator scapulae, and rhomboids are the major agonist muscles, found in the scapulothoratic joint, that allow the body to perform a push-up. The anterior deltoid, supraspinatus, and pectoralis major are all found in the glenohumeral joint. The biceps and triceps are agonists of the elbow joint.

9. C: Capping is a term used to describe the cease of a program prior to reaching the end goal. This may be done because the end goal has been deemed unrealistic, the current gains have been good enough, or the small gains between a current ability and the goal are not necessary for success. For example, a client with an original goal that was a very high 1RM on the bench press but who has decided to focus more effort on lower extremity training, even though he or she has not reached the 1RM goal.

10. A: A normal reading for triglycerides is <150 mg/dl; 150 to 199 is borderline high; 200 to 499 is high; and ≥500 is considered very high.

11. D: A personal trainer should never recommend supplements to a client; any nutritional advice beyond the scope of practice of a personal trainer should be referred to a licensed nutritionist. Supplements are not regulated by the FDA, and supplement manufacturing companies usually do not carry insurance, leaving the trainer liable to any implications of supplement recommendation or misuse. Additionally, underlying medical conditions such as heart disease or diabetes can be worsened by supplement use; use in these cases could lead to severe injury or death.

12. A: Progressive overload is the continual increase of stimuli to encourage growth, strength, and endurance. Prioritization and variation in training are other principles of specificity but do not consist of any specific level of intensity or frequency; they are differentiated by timing of stimuli and organization of the training program. Overload is specifically applying beyond the current adaptations of the body.

13. B: The Rockport 1-mile Walk Test is ideal for unconditioned individuals new to fitness or unable to run due to injury or a low fitness level. The 1.5-Mile Test is contraindicated for beginners and the unconditioned due to risk of injury. The Queens College Step Test and Astrand-Rhyming Test are 3 and 6 minutes in length, respectively, and are therefore not ideal for those just returning to fitness.

14. A: A personal trainer should hold, at a minimum, $1 million of professional liability insurance. This is considered the industry standard.

15. D: Behavior change is hindered by many things; the ability to change, scheduling, readiness, self-efficacy, scheduling, peer influence, and motivation are just a few. The cost, however, is a secondary conflict as changing one's behavior does not cost any money. The cost of a personal trainer, the cost of a gym membership, and so on, may be influences in the decision to change, but the cost itself is usually used to mask a lack of motivation, low self-efficacy, or insufficient readiness.

16. A: A personal trainer can refer clients to public websites such as MyPyramid.com and the Academy of Nutrition and Dietetics to share this information and help clients interpret the information found there. Any meal planning or nutrient supplementation should be referred to a licensed nutritionist or dietician.

17. B: Self-efficacy, an individual belief in one's own success, and the expectation of outcomes are the principles of the Social Cognitive Theory. Motivation is a person's mental drive toward behavior change, and extrinsic motivation is the drive coming from an outside source such as a change in appearance. Goal setting is a separate behavioral change theory that depends on the defining of personal goals and creating a plan to reach them.

18. C: Daily flexibility exercise is most the most effective for adults and at least 10 minutes of stretching is recommended. At a minimum, stretching exercises should be included in exercise programming 2 to 3 days each week.

19. B: The lumbar curve is made up of five vertebrae. The cervical curve consists of seven vertebrae, and the thoracic curve is 15 vertebrae.

20. C: This client is at the action stage of change. During the action stage, a person has a plan of action and is actively making behavior changes; however, he or she has been doing so for less than 6 months. The contemplation stage is during the time when a client is thinking about change and plans to do so in the future (within 6 months). During the preparation stage, the client has decided on a plan of action and will be beginning changes in behavior within the next 30 days. A client has reached the maintenance stage when he or she has been participating in behavior change for at least 6 months.

21. C: A person whose goal is to lose weight and decrease body fat should decrease his or her daily caloric intake by 500-1,000 kcals.

22. A: The baseline recommendation for moderate intensity cardiorespiratory training is at least 30 minutes per day on at least 5 days per week for a total of at least 150 minutes each week. Although any activity is better than none, it is recommended that an apparently healthy person participate in aerobic exercise between 3 to 5 days each week, with a combination of moderate and vigorous intensity levels.

23. A: Social support has been shown to be a key element in program adherence and is an important coping strategy in preventing relapse. Individuals with a strong support network, and whose family and friends are involved in their program, have greater success than those who do not. Assertiveness is the straightforward and honest expression of thoughts. Self-regulation is a client's ability to control his or her own behaviors, schedules, priorities, and so on. Intrinsic motivation is not a coping strategy but is the internal motivation of a person to adhere to the program for the sake of personal satisfaction and not because of the positive response of an external stimuli.

24. B: Motivational interviewing is a behavior-change technique in which the interviewer counsels the interviewee to find their own reasons to make a change. It involves empathy, active listening, asking open-ended questions, and building rapport with the client. Using motivational interviewing is far more effective in changing a client's behavior than any of these techniques alone because it can help the client to actually want to participate rather than doing so merely because they know rationally that they should or to appease someone else.

25. B: The success of active listening hinges on both verbal and nonverbal feedback from the listener to portray understanding and attention. During active listening, the listener accepts what the speaker is saying at face value and trusts it to be true. Rapport is a positive result of effective communication. Facial expressions are a form of nonverbal communication and can be used to express feedback to the speaker.

26. C: Systolic blood pressure ≥ 140 mmHg is a positive risk factor, not the listed reading of 135 mmHg. All other choices are positive health risk factors according to the guidelines set forth by ACSM.

27. A: The only negative risk factor in the ACSM risk stratification is a high-serum HDL cholesterol of ≥ 60 mg/dl. The three other available choices are all positive risk factors when listed on the medical history form.

28. C: SMART goals are specific, measurable, attainable, relevant, and time-bound.

29. B: A SMART goal must be specific, measurable, attainable, relevant, and time-bound. Choice A is not attainable as it is unrealistic to expect to lose 20 lbs. in 1 month of training. Choice C is nonspecific and is not measurable. Choice D is specific but not measurable.

30. A: This client is at the precontemplation stage of change, per transtheoretical modeling (TTM) of behavior change. During the precontemplation stage, the client is not yet ready to make change and is not motivated by the benefits of change now. During the contemplation stage of change, the client is aware of the negative effects of the behavior and is considering change within the next 6 months. Both the preparation and action stages of change come after the client has a relationship with a personal trainer and a plan of action.

31. C: The Health Belief Model is a theoretical approach in which the client must believe he or she can change, and the benefits of change are not outweighed by the barriers to change. Clients can be predicted to change based on their perceived seriousness of the negative consequences of their current state and their belief in a decreased risk of consequences as a result of change.

32. D: The most successful goals are those that are self-monitored by the client, follow the goal-setting strategies of SMART goals, and client-selected. Goals should not be flexible; they should be specific, measurable, attainable, realistic, and time oriented to ensure accurate monitoring.

33. A: The universally accepted body position, for reference, is the anatomical position. It is described as the body being erect with the arms at the sides, palms facing forward with thumbs pointed away from the body, and fingers extended.

34. A: The glenohumeral (shoulder) joint is a synovial ball-and-socket joint.

35. D: The lunge is an exercise that requires the agonist muscles—adductor longus, brevis, magus, gracilis, and pectineus—to perform adduction of the hip muscle. The leg raise requires flexion, and the machine hip abduction requires abduction of the hip joint. The broomstick twist is an exercise that performs rotation at the lumbar spine.

36. B: Glenoid fossa is not a joint; it is the depression of one bone into which another bone fits, forming a joint. The scapulothoratic joint provides stability and mobility for the orientation of the glenoid fossa while causing movement in the acromioclavicular, glenohumeral, and sternoclavicular joints.

37. A: An anterior pelvic tilt will increase lordosis in the lumbar spine. A posterior pelvic tilt will decrease lordosis in the spine. Both adduction of scapulae and scapular winging are deviations in shoulder position, whereas lordosis is a pelvic deviation.

38. B: Hypertrophy is the muscular adaptation to resistance training resulting in increased muscle size and strength. Atrophy refers to a reduction in muscle size, usually due to immobilization (injury) or inactivity. Endurance is a cardiorespiratory adaptation, and hyperplasia is an enlargement of tissue or an organ. It is caused by an increase in reproduction of cells and is often the initial stage in cancer development.

39. B: The body composition assessment would logically follow the resting heart rate and blood pressure measurements. This assessment is used to establish an optimal, desirable, or target weight for an individual as well as set solid height-weight and body mass index (BMI) reference points to be used during progress checks and reevaluation.

40. C: A male or female with a BMI between 18.5 and 24.9 is considered in the normal range.

41. D: A physician's medical clearance is required for any client with CAD. A personal trainer should not work with a client who has a preexisting condition until receiving input from the client's physician, and the trainer will follow the guidelines set by the physician. Regular programming cannot continue with a person who has CAD until clearance is given by a qualified physician. It is imperative that a personal trainer obtains the clearance in writing, along with the Release of Liability and Informed Consent.

42. A: Exercise, specifically weight-bearing and impact activities, promote bone health and strengthening. Enhanced feeling of well-being, improved cognitive function, and a decrease in anxiety and depression are all psychological benefits of exercise.

43. C: An older adult who follows a regular exercise program can expect to have a decreased risk of falls and experience an improvement of cognitive function. Both aerobic and resistance training has been shown to reduce the risk of dementia and other age-related declines in cognitive function. An increased metabolic rate, positive effect on stress, and weight loss are all benefits of exercise; however, they are not specific to any special population.

44. B: Fatigue is a normal result of exertion, especially at the start of an exercise program. Unusual fatigue or shortness of breath, syncope (dizziness), ankle edema, and orthopnea are all major signs or symptoms that suggest the presence of more serious diseases. Clients who exhibit these symptoms should be referred to a physician.

45. D: A client who has sporadic bouts of activity but no clear training plan are assigned the "Intermediate" activity status. The aerobic training plan for an intermediate client is to focus on moderate activity and aim for 200 to 300 minutes per week (fair to average fitness). The beginner status with either no prior or minimal activity is assigned to those who are completely inactive or deconditioned.

46. C: Because of the risk of orthostatic hypotension due to the possible obstruction of venous return in the supine position, pregnant women should avoid resistance and flexibility training in this position after the first trimester. The prone position is safe for pregnant women up until and after 6 weeks.

47. D: A client with diabetes should always check his or her blood glucose level prior to exercise and eat a snack if the reading is less than 100 mg/dl.

48. A: Sprint, plyometric, strength, and ballistic training are the best ways to improve an athlete's stride rate and frequency. This comprehensive approach helps the trained athlete to increase acceleration, enhance maximal speed and endurance, and strengthen the lower body.

49. B: At higher altitudes, air contains less oxygen than at sea level. Because there is less pressure to force the reduced oxygen into the blood, it is unable to deliver as much oxygen to the lungs as it would with higher levels of oxygen. While the pressure, density, and temperature are all different at various altitudes, the lightheadedness experienced by the exerciser is a direct result from a lack of oxygen.

50. C: The linear periodization is a classic method that uses a 1- to 4-week micro-cycle to time an increase in intensity and volume. A reverse linear program is beneficial to clients looking to achieve muscular endurance, but it follows the linear periodization in reverse order. A nonlinear program deviates from the classic periodization and usually uses a 12-week mesocycle. Progressive overload refers only to the increase in weight during resistance training.

51. A: Dynamic stretching is appropriate for use during the, and as a form of, warm-up because it involves the movement of body parts through their full range of motion by gradually increasing intensity. PNF, static, and passive stretching are only appropriate after a thorough warm-up of at least 5 to 10 minutes of light to moderate multi-joint, large muscle group movements. PNF should also only be performed by certified fitness professionals if they have been properly educated on the technique.

52. B: The cooldown portion of the training session should be between 5 and 10 minutes in length, depending on the client and the intensity of the active phase of training. It begins with a slow decrease in activity and concludes prior to the final flexibility and abdominal work.

53. C: The Valsalva maneuver is performed by trying to forcefully push inhaled air out through a closed mouth and obstructed nasal passage. It is essentially the "bearing down" of one's breath such as techniques used to "pop" a person's ears during an airplane descent, and it works by decreasing the preload pressure to the heart. As a result, however, it increases pressure in the abdominal cavity, which can further injure a client suffering from a hernia. Times breathing is a typical strategy used in exercise and is safe for all individuals. Pranayama and yogic breathing are the same technique, both used in yoga as slow, controlled inhalations and exhalations.

54. B: A client will lose strength and changes in muscle size at a rate of one-half the rate it was gained. For example, a client who increases his or her bench press by 50 percent over the course of 10 weeks will lose half that strength gain in 10 weeks and all of that gain in 20 weeks.

55. D: A spotter should always assist any time the client's speed decreases. The spotter should also always keep hands as close to the weights as possible while not obstructing the movement, always use collard or clips on an evenly loaded bar, and communicate to the client how many repetitions remain in each set.

56. C: A client who has improper form during a certain movement would most benefit from visual cues (shown on your own body), wrong-right cues (moving your own body in and out of the correct position), and tactile cues (using a hands-on method) to correct the form. Imagery is best used in yoga or meditation to elicit an emotion or thought in the client. Safety cues are informational but would not be the best way to describe a corrective motion. Affirmational or motivational cues are used as encouragement and to energize.

57. C: Weight lifting should be performed in smooth, continuous motions using the correct grip, with a tight, engaged core, proper body positioning, and the weight held close to the body to avoid injury.

58. B: SAID is a common specificity principle that calls for programming that causes adaptations within the body that will be specific to the demands of the goal. Prioritization is often used opposite a competitive season schedule and trains one aspect of muscular fitness at a time, and resistance training refers to a combination of consecutive training sessions. Cardiovascular prioritization is not a specificity principle.

59. D: Pronation of the foot causes the ankles to collapse inward, and abduction of the knee is an internal rotation between the femur and tibia. This causes valgus stress and increases strain on the anterior cruciate ligament (ACL).

60. A: The medical history form is used for screening purposes and identifies metabolic, cardiovascular, pulmonary, musculoskeletal, or other client problems. Although the PARQ is another medical screening tool, it does not identify CHD risk factors. The informed consent form is a signed acknowledgement of the possible risks involved in participating in the activity, and the physician's clearance form is used after risks have been identified and assists in program design.

61. C: The amount of hip flexion required to perform the squat averages approximately 95 degrees. The hips typically flex between 100 and 135 degrees with a full range of motion.

62. B: The hip hinge is an exercise in a functional training progression that promotes glute dominance over quad dominance when performing a squat. A lower-extremity alignment and bend-and-lift screen would promote hip alignment over the hips, knees, and feet and determine if the client requires hip abductor or adductor strengthening and/or stretching. The figure-four position is one that promotes alignment between the tibia and truck.

63. A: Hopscotch, skipping, and jumping are activities that encourage bone strengthening because of the force they place on the developing bones of children. Tug-of-war and tree climbing are examples of muscle-strengthening activities. Walking and bicycle riding are moderate-intensity aerobic activities for children, and swimming and skiing are vigorous-intensity aerobic activities.

64. B: The correct progression for performing bilateral and unilateral chest presses is seated press, standing press, single-arm press with contralateral stance, and single-arm with ipsilateral stance

65. A: The correct progression of the wood chop exercise when training rotational movement is the long moment arm, standing short moment arm, standing long moment arm, hip hinge/squat, long moment arm, and full chop.

66. B: Positive reinforcement is communicated using verbal (praise) and nonverbal (eye contact and empathy) cues that create a positive experience for the client. Stimulus control and shaping are also operant conditioning tools. Shaping is the process of gradually increasing the demands of a skill the client already has to help him or her achieve a desired behavior. Stimulus control refers to the altering of the cause of an action to change the outcome of the situation. Behavior chains are series of responses to stimuli that can either lead to or avoid desired behaviors.

67. C: The whole-part-whole teaching method helps the trainer give clear and specific instructions on how to perform a new movement. The trainer should identify the movement, demonstrate the movement (whole), detail the exercise by breaking down the parts of the movement, and demonstrate it a second time (whole) before cuing the client to begin.

68. A: The exercise continuum is a scale from left (1) to right (6) that is used to rate the difficulty of an exercise. A client who cannot perform a given movement must have the exercise moved to the left (modified) to decrease difficulty.

69. B: Feedback is an essential part of goal setting and an important component of behavior change. Feedback is defined as two-way communication, is imperative for effective self-monitoring, and should be strongly encouraged at the onset of a new program, especially with a new, unfamiliar client. Positive reinforcement is a motivational tactic, intervention is used with a person who has not yet decided on a behavior change, and customization is completed on an ongoing basis through any normal programming.

70. C: The Social Cognitive Theory is based on the Health Belief Model and states that what a person thinks may happen (expectations) and self-efficacy are the most important factors in behavior change. The Health Belief Model states that a client must believe the health benefits of behavior change outweigh the barriers to change. Goal Setting Theory is moderated by the level of commitment to change, and the Theory of Planned Behavior states that a person's intention to engage in a certain behavior will ultimately lead to that behavior.

71. C: Dyslipidemia is the elevated measurements of LDL cholesterol and total cholesterol.

72. B: Forty grams of carbohydrate at 4 calories per gram, 16 grams of protein at 4 calories per gram, and 9 grams of fat at 9 calories per gram equal a total of 305 calories: (40 x 4) + (16 x 4) + (9 x 9) = 305.

73. C: Weight fluctuations of 10 or more pounds, depressed mood, obsession with one's appearance, disturbance of body image (claiming to "feel fat"), and severely restrictive diets are all signs and symptoms of an eating disorder. Personal trainers do not diagnose disorders; this client should be referred to a health care professional.

74. D: The recommendation for fluid consumption and hydration for exercisers is to consume approximately 500 mL of fluid about 2 hours before exercising. During exercise, a person should consume fluid at regular intervals and at the same rate of water loss though sweating.

75. C: Female Athlete Triad is characterized by a decrease in bone mineral density with or without osteoporosis, energy imbalances with or without eating disorders, and menstrual disturbances.

76. D: One gram of carbohydrates is 4 kcals, or 4 calories. One gram of protein is also 4 kcals, and 1 gram of fat is 9 kcals.

77. C: Despite the fact that unorganized or busy clients, or those with poor time-management skills, are more prone to relapse, regulating that client's schedule eliminates the important lapse deterrent of self-regulation. Clients should be taught to self-monitor and make their own behavioral changes to maximize success in fitness programming.

78. A: Increasing muscle mass requires consuming a caloric surplus. However, the number of excess calories to be consumed when training for hypertrophy is variable and depends on the client's metabolism, height, current weight, and several other factors. Clients training to increase muscle mass should also perform muscle-building exercises and consume adequate amounts of both macronutrients (including increased protein) and micronutrients.

79. B: Eating smaller, more frequent meals has been shown to maintain metabolic rate, but it does not cause a change to the metabolic rate such as an increase or decrease. This style of eating also helps lower body fat and lower weight on high caloric intakes, maintain muscle mass and better glucose tolerance, improve physical performance, and lower stress hormone production.

80. A: A client whose weight is 210 lbs. with 21 percent body fat has a lean body mass weighing 166 lbs.: 210 x 0.21 = 44.1 lbs. (body fat); 210 – 44.1 lbs. = 165.9 lbs. (lean mass).

81. B: Tort law is the theory of law that regulates civil wrongdoing. There is an area of tort law called "premises liability," which states it is the trainer's responsibility to maintain a safe premise and ensure the safety of the client while training. Malpractice refers to wrongdoing by licensed professionals such as doctors and surgeons. Negligence is the law itself that is upheld by the theory of tort law, and liability is the responsibility the trainer accepts in keeping clients safe.

82. B: A CPR micro-shield is a pliable, plastic shield designed to cover the victim's mouth while performing mouth-to-mask ventilation, also known as protected mouth-to-mouth resuscitation. Mouth-to-mouth resuscitation should be avoided in the public setting to avoid direct contact with the victim's mouth. Automated external defibrillation is performed using an automated external defibrillator in the emergency procedures of cardiac arrest.

83. A: The whole-part-whole teaching method follows the same procedure as the demo-detail-demo teaching method.

84. A: Removing the machine from the gym floor is the only way to completely remove the additional risk of harm or injury from attempting to use a malfunctioning machine. When it is safe, excuse yourself from your client to remove the machine, or recruit other staff members to remove it. An "out of order" sign does not remove the risk from attempting to use the broken machine. It also allows for the sign to be removed, moved, or unable to be read during daily tasks around the machine. Although you should never leave a client mid-exercise and should wait until he or she has finished performing the movement, you should not wait until after the session is complete to remove the risk. Unplugging the machine creates the additional risk of the loose cord.

85. C: ITBS is an overuse injury that causes pain along the outside of the thigh down to the knee. Lateral epicondylitis is another name for "tennis elbow"; tendinitis is an inflammatory response in the tendons caused by a new, increased level of demand on tendons.

86. D: A fracture is a break or disruption in the continuation of bone; they are deemed either "open" or "closed" depending on whether the broken bone pushes through the skin after injury. A sprain is an injury caused by the twisting of a body joint. A strain is a stretch or tear in muscle fibers, such as a tendon or fascia. Hypoxia is an injury caused by when a person stops breathing during a seizure.

87. C: Movement to the right on the exercise continuum, or increasing the difficulty of a given exercise, is called "progression" and is done when a given movement becomes too easy. Progression is achieved by increasing repetitions, increasing weight, increasing the speed of an exercise, or any combination of progressions.

88. C: The four major types of shock (hypoperfusion) are obstructive, hypovolemic, distributive, and cardiogenic.

89. B: A grade II strain is a moderate strain. A grade I strain is considered mild in which only a few fibers are stretched and possibly torn. A grade II strain is classified as a complete tear resulting in complete loss of muscle function.

90. A: The lateral and medial menisci perform the functions of shock absorption, proprioception, lubrication, stability, and joint congruency. The ACL and MCL are ligaments crossing the front of knee, and each performs a separate function. The patella is another name for the knee cap and has a thin layer of cartilage beneath it to prevent the bones from rubbing together.

91. B: An independent contractor is usually hired on a short-term or temporary basis. This arrangement is popular among personal trainers because it allows trainers to choose their own clients, make their own schedules, and work for more than one employer at a given time. A salaried employee would be a full-time, regular employee of the facility. This arrangement is considered long-term, and during the time of employment, the employer sets the trainer's hours, controls the fees charged, and maintains control over the trainer-client relationship.

92. C: The charge of negligence is an accusation that a trainer failed to uphold the standard of care necessary to perform his job; the damage does not need to be directly caused by the trainer.

93. B: The Family Educational Rights and Privacy Act (FERPA protects the privacy of students and their educational records. The USDHHS is the United States Department of Health and Human Services. Health Insurance Portability and Accountability Act (HIPAA) is a privacy act protecting victims and the privacy of their health records. The USDoE is the US Department of Education.

94. A: A decisional balance exercise helps a client determine the positives and negatives of behavior change and is used in conjunction with the TTM. Cognitive and behavioral strategies are used to combine stages of change and the process of change in the TTM.

95. D: Short-term disability insurance is sold separately from professional liability insurance and is mostly marketed toward health care providers. Professional liability insurance covers claims such as those arising from breach of contract, negligence, damages to property, injury to persons, and even sexual harassment.

96. C: Copyright laws prohibit you from using music, recordings, and broadcasts without first purchasing licenses to do so. While in a client's home, have clients provide their own music so that its use is noncommercial and for his or her own private enjoyment.

97. B: An insurance rider is a special addition to current insurance provisions and can cover activities such as training clients outdoors, in their homes, or in your private residence. Although incorporation has its own benefits, it is not required to operate a business out of your home. Business licenses and permits do not limit advertisement, and housing standards do not require a separate business entrance for in-home operated businesses, although you should always check with your local housing council for special considerations.

98. A: An increase in repetitions, even for beginners, will create faster improvements in technique and strength. While single sets may be enough for the most inexperienced clients to see results, they are not the most efficient way to progress at any level. A client should always increase repetitions and reach a maximum number of repetitions and sets before increasing weight loads. When teaching a new skill to a client, a trainer should always begin with no additional weight added until the client has mastered the balance and achieve the strength needed to complete the weighted exercise safely.

99. D: Spinal twists and spinal extensions are thoracic spine (T-spine) mobilization exercises. The supine 90-90 hip rotator stretch improves hip mobility in the transverse plane, the shoulder bridge improves hip mobilization with glute activation, and rocking quadrupeds are for posterior mobilization.

100. C: Individuals who have two or more risk factors are considered to be a moderate risk. Clients with zero or one risk factor are considered low risk, and any client with a known cardiovascular, pulmonary, or metabolic disease is automatically high risk.

101. D: A decrease in maximum minute ventilation is a physiological adaptation of aerobic conditioning at submaximal effort. At maximal effort, maximum minute ventilation can be expected to increase.

102. B: Shaping is the behavioral change tactic that uses reinforcements to achieve a target behavior. Observational learning is the influence a person's environment has on his or her ability to make a change, and stimulus control is adjustments made to a person's environment that either increase or decrease the likelihood of healthy behaviors. Extinction is the removal of a positive stimulus that once existed following a behavior, and it decreases the likelihood that the behavior will be repeated.

103. A: HIPAA was enacted as a federal law in 1996. It puts the victim in complete control over who has access to his or her health information; anyone who is to view or discuss private client information must be given explicit permission by the client.

104. B: Shin splints are an overuse injury causing pain in the lower, anterior leg. ITBS is shown along the outside of the knee and thigh. Bursitis is caused by inflammation of the bursa sac, and lateral epicondylitis is the medical term for "tennis elbow."

105. A: Increased resting heart rate, disturbed sleep, and decreased hunger are all signs of overtraining. A client exhibiting these symptoms should be encouraged to provide more time for recovery and decrease frequency and/or decrease intensity of training sessions.

106. C: A LLC is protected under the veil of corporation, which creates a separate legal identity responsible for any liabilities and filing taxes as its own entity. A sole proprietorship is a business owned by a single person, whose business finances and liabilities are tied up with his or her personal finances, including tax filing. A partnership operates as a sole proprietorship with more than one owner. An express partnership is a type of partnership, an express, implied, or minority agreement, among others.

107. B: Purging-type behaviors to prevent weight gain are not a characteristic of binge-eating disorder. Purging is a characteristic of bulimia nervosa.

108. A: Keyman insurance is sold to businesses owned and operated by more than once person and is designed to cover the loss of a person who performs a valuable and unique function; this person is not easily replaced, and the company would suffer great financial hardship at his or her loss. Umbrella insurance is added insurance for any liability policy. Product liability insurance is to protect a facility from a faulty product, and disability insurance is recommended for any company wishing to protect themselves from disability claims from employees.

109. C: This client is most likely suffering from DOMS. This injury manifests within 24 to 48 hours after exercise and can last anywhere from 5 to 7 days. DOMS is a sign of pushing oneself too hard, too soon, and it should never be the goal of a workout as it is not a measure of how hard a client has worked. Muscle strains and sprains are injuries that will show themselves immediately after the injury has occurred. Sprains are often accompanied by a tearing or pop sound and sudden pain. Exhaustion is a level of tiredness.

110. A: The lean mass percentage of a client with a body fat percentage of 17 percent is 83 percent: 100 – 17% = 83%.

111. A: The MCL is responsible for preventing medial bending on the knee. The ACL's primary purpose is to prevent anterior glide of the tibia, separating it from the femur. The PCL is the posterior cruciate ligament, and the meniscus is a soft layer of cushion protecting the femur and tibia.

112. B: The sagittal plane divides the body into right and left sides. The frontal plane divides the body in posterior and anterior portions and is also called the coronal plane. The transverse plane, also called the axial, cross-sectional, or horizontal plane, divides the body into superior and inferior portions.

113. D: An effective communicator should always avoid using metaphors or slang. The fourth element of active listening is to understand contextual anxiety.

114. A: Body composition is the term used to describe a body's ratio of lean body mass to body fat. Body fat percentage is specifically what percentage of a person's body is fat. BMI is used to assess weight relative to one's height. Body fat distribution is a term used to describe where on the body a person holds the most fat.

115. A: Risk management is a process through which a business uses foreseeability to minimize health risks and liability issues. As a personal trainer, this includes CPR, AED, and first aid training, the creation of an emergency response plan, and written emergency procedures that include when to call 911 and the use of automated defibrillators. An IPO is the initial public offering of company shares to potential, public shareholders. The accountability structure is a defined list of responsibilities and to whom each responsibility falls. Audits are a common business practice that involves the testing and evaluating of company procedures and, more commonly, bookkeeping.

116. D: About 65 percent of the population is visual learners and will benefit most from first being shown how to perform a movement. The most effective trainers use a combination of all three learning types along with the proper cuing.

117. D: The release of liability is an added level of liability protection and is an agreement between the client and trainer and/or facility that the participant relinquishes his or her rights to collect damages in the case of injury. Both the PARQ and medical history forms are used as screening tools, and a self-assessment quiz is used to help clients understand their own levels of wellness.

118. D: The adrenal gland is responsible for production of cortisol, also known as the stress hormone. Mind-body exercise such as yoga as well as stress reducing activities help reduce the cortisol produced by the adrenal gland, therefore lowering stress levels. The apocrine, eccrine, and sebaceous glands are all located on the skin and are sweat glands.

119. B: Men require between 2 and 5 percent body fat, and women require between 10 and 13 percent body fat to maintain normal body function and overall health. Lower body fat will inhibit its functions of hormone production, insulation, cushioning of vital organs, thermoregulation, and maintenance of other certain body functions.

120. D: Clients who are deemed to be moderate risk require a medical exam prior to vigorous exercise. Doctor supervision during submaximal testing and a medical exam before moderate exercise are required only for high risk clients. Clients with one risk factor are considered low risk.

121. D: Five grams of fat contain 45 calories, greater than the carbohydrate and protein total calorie contributions at 4 calories per gram for each. Fiber is not a macronutrient but a micronutrient included in carbohydrates.

How to Overcome Test Anxiety

Just the thought of taking a test is enough to make most people a little nervous. A test is an important event that can have a long-term impact on your future, so it's important to take it seriously and it's natural to feel anxious about performing well. But just because anxiety is normal, that doesn't mean that it's helpful in test taking, or that you should simply accept it as part of your life. Anxiety can have a variety of effects. These effects can be mild, like making you feel slightly nervous, or severe, like blocking your ability to focus or remember even a simple detail.

If you experience test anxiety—whether severe or mild—it's important to know how to beat it. To discover this, first you need to understand what causes test anxiety.

Causes of Test Anxiety

While we often think of anxiety as an uncontrollable emotional state, it can actually be caused by simple, practical things. One of the most common causes of test anxiety is that a person does not feel adequately prepared for their test. This feeling can be the result of many different issues such as poor study habits or lack of organization, but the most common culprit is time management. Starting to study too late, failing to organize your study time to cover all of the material, or being distracted while you study will mean that you're not well prepared for the test. This may lead to cramming the night before, which will cause you to be physically and mentally exhausted for the test. Poor time management also contributes to feelings of stress, fear, and hopelessness as you realize you are not well prepared but don't know what to do about it.

Other times, test anxiety is not related to your preparation for the test but comes from unresolved fear. This may be a past failure on a test, or poor performance on tests in general. It may come from comparing yourself to others who seem to be performing better or from the stress of living up to expectations. Anxiety may be driven by fears of the future—how failure on this test would affect your educational and career goals. These fears are often completely irrational, but they can still negatively impact your test performance.

Elements of Test Anxiety

As mentioned earlier, test anxiety is considered to be an emotional state, but it has physical and mental components as well. Sometimes you may not even realize that you are suffering from test anxiety until you notice the physical symptoms. These can include trembling hands, rapid heartbeat, sweating, nausea, and tense muscles. Extreme anxiety may lead to fainting or vomiting. Obviously, any of these symptoms can have a negative impact on testing. It is important to recognize them as soon as they begin to occur so that you can address the problem before it damages your performance.

The mental components of test anxiety include trouble focusing and inability to remember learned information. During a test, your mind is on high alert, which can help you recall information and stay focused for an extended period of time. However, anxiety interferes with your mind's natural processes, causing you to blank out, even on the questions you know well. The strain of testing during anxiety makes it difficult to stay focused, especially on a test that may take several hours. Extreme anxiety can take a huge mental toll, making it difficult not only to recall test information but even to understand the test questions or pull your thoughts together.

Effects of Test Anxiety

Test anxiety is like a disease—if left untreated, it will get progressively worse. Anxiety leads to poor performance, and this reinforces the feelings of fear and failure, which in turn lead to poor performances on subsequent tests. It can grow from a mild nervousness to a crippling condition. If allowed to progress, test anxiety can have a big impact on your schooling, and consequently on your future.

Test anxiety can spread to other parts of your life. Anxiety on tests can become anxiety in any stressful situation, and blanking on a test can turn into panicking in a job situation. But fortunately, you don't have to let anxiety rule your testing and determine your grades. There are a number of relatively simple steps you can take to move past anxiety and function normally on a test and in the rest of life.

Physical Steps for Beating Test Anxiety

While test anxiety is a serious problem, the good news is that it can be overcome. It doesn't have to control your ability to think and remember information. While it may take time, you can begin taking steps today to beat anxiety.

Just as your first hint that you may be struggling with anxiety comes from the physical symptoms, the first step to treating it is also physical. Rest is crucial for having a clear, strong mind. If you are tired, it is much easier to give in to anxiety. But if you establish good sleep habits, your body and mind will be ready to perform optimally, without the strain of exhaustion. Additionally, sleeping well helps you to retain information better, so you're more likely to recall the answers when you see the test questions.

Getting good sleep means more than going to bed on time. It's important to allow your brain time to relax. Take study breaks from time to time so it doesn't get overworked, and don't study right before bed. Take time to rest your mind before trying to rest your body, or you may find it difficult to fall asleep.

Along with sleep, other aspects of physical health are important in preparing for a test. Good nutrition is vital for good brain function. Sugary foods and drinks may give a burst of energy but this burst is followed by a crash, both physically and emotionally. Instead, fuel your body with protein and vitamin-rich foods.

Also, drink plenty of water. Dehydration can lead to headaches and exhaustion, especially if your brain is already under stress from the rigors of the test. Particularly if your test is a long one, drink water during the breaks. And if possible, take an energy-boosting snack to eat between sections.

Along with sleep and diet, a third important part of physical health is exercise. Maintaining a steady workout schedule is helpful, but even taking 5-minute study breaks to walk can help get your blood pumping faster and clear your head. Exercise also releases endorphins, which contribute to a positive feeling and can help combat test anxiety.

When you nurture your physical health, you are also contributing to your mental health. If your body is healthy, your mind is much more likely to be healthy as well. So take time to rest, nourish your body with healthy food and water, and get moving as much as possible. Taking these physical steps will make you stronger and more able to take the mental steps necessary to overcome test anxiety.

Mental Steps for Beating Test Anxiety

Working on the mental side of test anxiety can be more challenging, but as with the physical side, there are clear steps you can take to overcome it. As mentioned earlier, test anxiety often stems from lack of preparation, so the obvious solution is to prepare for the test. Effective studying may be the most important weapon you have for beating test anxiety, but you can and should employ several other mental tools to combat fear.

First, boost your confidence by reminding yourself of past success—tests or projects that you aced. If you're putting as much effort into preparing for this test as you did for those, there's no reason you should expect to fail here. Work hard to prepare; then trust your preparation.

Second, surround yourself with encouraging people. It can be helpful to find a study group, but be sure that the people you're around will encourage a positive attitude. If you spend time with others who are anxious or cynical, this will only contribute to your own anxiety. Look for others who are motivated to study hard from a desire to succeed, not from a fear of failure.

Third, reward yourself. A test is physically and mentally tiring, even without anxiety, and it can be helpful to have something to look forward to. Plan an activity following the test, regardless of the outcome, such as going to a movie or getting ice cream.

When you are taking the test, if you find yourself beginning to feel anxious, remind yourself that you know the material. Visualize successfully completing the test. Then take a few deep, relaxing breaths and return to it. Work through the questions carefully but with confidence, knowing that you are capable of succeeding.

Developing a healthy mental approach to test taking will also aid in other areas of life. Test anxiety affects more than just the actual test—it can be damaging to your mental health and even contribute to depression. It's important to beat test anxiety before it becomes a problem for more than testing.

Study Strategy

Being prepared for the test is necessary to combat anxiety, but what does being prepared look like? You may study for hours on end and still not feel prepared. What you need is a strategy for test prep. The next few pages outline our recommended steps to help you plan out and conquer the challenge of preparation.

Step 1: Scope Out the Test

Learn everything you can about the format (multiple choice, essay, etc.) and what will be on the test. Gather any study materials, course outlines, or sample exams that may be available. Not only will this help you to prepare, but knowing what to expect can help to alleviate test anxiety.

Step 2: Map Out the Material

Look through the textbook or study guide and make note of how many chapters or sections it has. Then divide these over the time you have. For example, if a book has 15 chapters and you have five days to study, you need to cover three chapters each day. Even better, if you have the time, leave an extra day at the end for overall review after you have gone through the material in depth.

If time is limited, you may need to prioritize the material. Look through it and make note of which sections you think you already have a good grasp on, and which need review. While you are studying, skim quickly through the familiar sections and take more time on the challenging parts.

Write out your plan so you don't get lost as you go. Having a written plan also helps you feel more in control of the study, so anxiety is less likely to arise from feeling overwhelmed at the amount to cover.

Step 3: Gather Your Tools

Decide what study method works best for you. Do you prefer to highlight in the book as you study and then go back over the highlighted portions? Or do you type out notes of the important information? Or is it helpful to make flashcards that you can carry with you? Assemble the pens, index cards, highlighters, post-it notes, and any other materials you may need so you won't be distracted by getting up to find things while you study.

If you're having a hard time retaining the information or organizing your notes, experiment with different methods. For example, try color-coding by subject with colored pens, highlighters, or post-it notes. If you learn better by hearing, try recording yourself reading your notes so you can listen while in the car, working out, or simply sitting at your desk. Ask a friend to quiz you from your flashcards, or try teaching someone the material to solidify it in your mind.

Step 4: Create Your Environment

It's important to avoid distractions while you study. This includes both the obvious distractions like visitors and the subtle distractions like an uncomfortable chair (or a too-comfortable couch that makes you want to fall asleep). Set up the best study environment possible: good lighting and a comfortable work area. If background music helps you focus, you may want to turn it on, but otherwise keep the room quiet. If you are using a computer to take notes, be sure you don't have any other windows open, especially applications like social media, games, or anything else that could distract you. Silence your phone and turn off notifications. Be sure to keep water close by so you stay hydrated while you study (but avoid unhealthy drinks and snacks).

Also, take into account the best time of day to study. Are you freshest first thing in the morning? Try to set aside some time then to work through the material. Is your mind clearer in the afternoon or evening? Schedule your study session then. Another method is to study at the same time of day that you will take the test, so that your brain gets used to working on the material at that time and will be ready to focus at test time.

Step 5: Study!

Once you have done all the study preparation, it's time to settle into the actual studying. Sit down, take a few moments to settle your mind so you can focus, and begin to follow your study plan. Don't give in to distractions or let yourself procrastinate. This is your time to prepare so you'll be ready to fearlessly approach the test. Make the most of the time and stay focused.

Of course, you don't want to burn out. If you study too long you may find that you're not retaining the information very well. Take regular study breaks. For example, taking five minutes out of every hour to walk briskly, breathing deeply and swinging your arms, can help your mind stay fresh.

As you get to the end of each chapter or section, it's a good idea to do a quick review. Remind yourself of what you learned and work on any difficult parts. When you feel that you've mastered the material, move on to the next part. At the end of your study session, briefly skim through your notes again.

But while review is helpful, cramming last minute is NOT. If at all possible, work ahead so that you won't need to fit all your study into the last day. Cramming overloads your brain with more information than it can process and retain, and your tired mind may struggle to recall even previously learned information when it is overwhelmed with last-minute study. Also, the urgent nature of cramming and the stress placed on your brain contribute to anxiety. You'll be more likely to go to the test feeling unprepared and having trouble thinking clearly.

So don't cram, and don't stay up late before the test, even just to review your notes at a leisurely pace. Your brain needs rest more than it needs to go over the information again. In fact, plan to finish your studies by noon or early afternoon the day before the test. Give your brain the rest of the day to relax or focus on other things, and get a good night's sleep. Then you will be fresh for the test and better able to recall what you've studied.

Step 6: Take a Practice Test

Many courses offer sample tests, either online or in the study materials. This is an excellent resource to check whether you have mastered the material, as well as to prepare for the test format and environment.

Check the test format ahead of time: the number of questions, the type (multiple choice, free response, etc.), and the time limit. Then create a plan for working through them. For example, if you have 30 minutes to take a 60-question test, your limit is 30 seconds per question. Spend less time on the questions you know well so that you can take more time on the difficult ones.

If you have time to take several practice tests, take the first one open book, with no time limit. Work through the questions at your own pace and make sure you fully understand them. Gradually work up to taking a test under test conditions: sit at a desk with all study materials put away and set a timer. Pace yourself to make sure you finish the test with time to spare and go back to check your answers if you have time.

After each test, check your answers. On the questions you missed, be sure you understand why you missed them. Did you misread the question (tests can use tricky wording)? Did you forget the information? Or was it something you hadn't learned? Go back and study any shaky areas that the practice tests reveal.

Taking these tests not only helps with your grade, but also aids in combating test anxiety. If you're already used to the test conditions, you're less likely to worry about it, and working through tests until you're scoring well gives you a confidence boost. Go through the practice tests until you feel comfortable, and then you can go into the test knowing that you're ready for it.

Test Tips

On test day, you should be confident, knowing that you've prepared well and are ready to answer the questions. But aside from preparation, there are several test day strategies you can employ to maximize your performance.

First, as stated before, get a good night's sleep the night before the test (and for several nights before that, if possible). Go into the test with a fresh, alert mind rather than staying up late to study.

Try not to change too much about your normal routine on the day of the test. It's important to eat a nutritious breakfast, but if you normally don't eat breakfast at all, consider eating just a protein bar. If you're a coffee drinker, go ahead and have your normal coffee. Just make sure you time it so that the caffeine doesn't wear off right in the middle of your test. Avoid sugary beverages, and drink enough water to stay hydrated but not so much that you need a restroom break 10 minutes into the test. If your test isn't first thing in the morning, consider going for a walk or doing a light workout before the test to get your blood flowing.

Allow yourself enough time to get ready, and leave for the test with plenty of time to spare so you won't have the anxiety of scrambling to arrive in time. Another reason to be early is to select a good seat. It's helpful to sit away from doors and windows, which can be distracting. Find a good seat, get out your supplies, and settle your mind before the test begins.

When the test begins, start by going over the instructions carefully, even if you already know what to expect. Make sure you avoid any careless mistakes by following the directions.

Then begin working through the questions, pacing yourself as you've practiced. If you're not sure on an answer, don't spend too much time on it, and don't let it shake your confidence. Either skip it and come back later, or eliminate as many wrong answers as possible and guess among the remaining ones. Don't dwell on these questions as you continue—put them out of your mind and focus on what lies ahead.

Be sure to read all of the answer choices, even if you're sure the first one is the right answer. Sometimes you'll find a better one if you keep reading. But don't second-guess yourself if you do immediately know the answer. Your gut instinct is usually right. Don't let test anxiety rob you of the information you know.

If you have time at the end of the test (and if the test format allows), go back and review your answers. Be cautious about changing any, since your first instinct tends to be correct, but make sure you didn't misread any of the questions or accidentally mark the wrong answer choice. Look over any you skipped and make an educated guess.

At the end, leave the test feeling confident. You've done your best, so don't waste time worrying about your performance or wishing you could change anything. Instead, celebrate the successful completion of this test. And finally, use this test to learn how to deal with anxiety even better next time.

Review Video: Test Anxiety
Visit mometrix.com/academy and enter code: 100340

Important Qualification

Not all anxiety is created equal. If your test anxiety is causing major issues in your life beyond the classroom or testing center, or if you are experiencing troubling physical symptoms related to your anxiety, it may be a sign of a serious physiological or psychological condition. If this sounds like your situation, we strongly encourage you to seek professional help.

Online Resources

Due to our efforts to try to keep this book to a manageable length, we've created a link that will give you access to all of your online resources:

mometrix.com/resources719/acsm

It's Your Moment, Let's Celebrate It!

Share your story @mometrixtestpreparation